THE PROPAGANDA SOCIETY

THE PROPAGANDA SOCIETY

JEAN-YVES LE GALLOU

RESISTANCE MANUAL FOR THE MENTAL GULAG

ARKTOS
LONDON 2025

ARKTOS

Arktos.com   fb.com/Arktos   arktosmedia   arktosjournal

Copyright © 2025 by Arktos Media Ltd. and La Nouvelle Librairie.

All rights reserved. No part of this book may be reproduced or utilised in any form or by any means (whether electronic or mechanical), including photocopying, recording or by any information storage and retrieval system, without permission in writing from the publisher.

La société de propagande: Manuel de résistance au goulag mental, published as part of the *Collection Cartouches* by La Nouvelle Librairie éditions in 2022.

ISBN
978-1-917646-60-4 (Paperback)
978-1-917646-62-8 (Hardback)
978-1-917646-61-1 (Ebook)

Translation
Roger Adwan

Editing
Constantin von Hoffmeister

Layout and Cover
Tor Westman

CONTENTS

Preamble: The Necessary Definition.......................... vii

I. Total Propaganda — Welcome to the Mental Gulag............1

II. Totalitarian Propaganda: The Great Entrapment of Minds.....19

III. From Secession to Reconquest............................51

❧

L'Institut Iliade for Long European Memory.................... 62

PREAMBLE

THE NECESSARY DEFINITION

When Julius Caesar published *The Gallic Wars*, he acted as much as a propagandist as a memoirist. The account of his exploits paved the way for his rise to power. When Suetonius wrote *The Lives of the Twelve Caesars*, he penned an entire vilification of the fallen Julio-Claudian and Flavian dynasties in order to better glorify the Antonine dynasty that had succeeded them: he thus sang the praise of the 'good emperors' (Machiavelli), of princes whose statues adorned the forums of the Empire's cities.

Much later, in 1622, the Church created the Congregation for the Propagation[1] of the Faith, thus fulfilling its vocation of conversion and control. For the sake of linguistic convenience, Pope Paul VI removed the word 'propagation' from the institution's name in 1967: only the word, of course, not the fact itself.

Why? Because today, the word has negative connotations and no one dares to use it anymore. The term 'communication' is the preferred choice, even if propaganda is one of the levers of power that allow one to ensure the unity of human societies. However, although propaganda

---

1   Translator's note (TN): Here, Jean-Yves Le Gallou uses the word *propagande*, meaning 'propaganda', although the prevailing French name is similar to the English one and includes the term 'propagation'.

is indeed an integral part of many human societies, it was far from being the sole element that ensured their unity and stability in the past. Traditional societies were framed by:

- religious faith;
- close village or middle-class ties;
- community life and festivals;
- the existence of human ideal types;
- codes of values.

Under these conditions, propaganda was perhaps not superfluous but, regardless of location among the deeply rooted men of traditional societies, at least in line with the social norms of the organic communities and based on their identity and particularities.

This is not the case in contemporary Western societies, where propaganda now plays the most prominent role — which is why, in accordance with Orwellian logic, the word has disappeared from people's 'appropriate' vocabulary. When organic bonds were dissolved in industrial societies, an entire apparatus of police and judicial repression developed, with prisons in democracies and concentration camps in totalitarian countries: propaganda in totalitarian countries and 'communication' in Western ones. Communication, really? It's nothing but a Newspeak term to designate different strategies of influence and mind control, especially since the 1914 war destroyed all that remained of the inherited order in traditional societies. And it is on the latter's ruins — as stated by Dominique Venner in *The Century of 1914* — that four ideologies have emerged and fought against each other: apart from Anglo-Saxon globalism, we are referring to fascism, National Socialism, and communism. All these ideologies, which have now vanished and are reviled posthumously, used propaganda and coercion to assert themselves. They did not, however, invent modern propaganda. Stalin and Goebbels were not the geniuses that some believe them to be. Modern propaganda was born at the end of the 19th century in American public relations firms and served the interests of the 'robber barons', the ancestors of the great oligarchs. The undisputed master of mind control was Edward Bernays. And his techniques, which are now more than a century old, are those that ensure more than ever before the prevalence of commodities over the entire world. A brilliant nephew of Sigmund Freund and a practitioner of 'public relations' in both the business world and American politics (whether domestic or foreign), Edward Bernays (1891–1995) died at the age of 104, having synthesised his thoughts and actions in a short work published in 1928 and simply entitled *Propaganda*, which presents us with a genuine description of the 'invisible government'. In it, he explains 'how to manipulate public opinion in a democracy'; hence the subtitle of his book in French.

According to Bernays, all this serves the common good: advertising thus allows a large company to create a vast market without which capitalism could not prosper, while providing the greatest possible number of people with access to consumer goods at a lower cost. The same advertising methods can be used to justify a 'just war', including the USA's involvement in World War I in 1917, despite the fact that American public opinion remained hostile to it for a very long time.

A postmodern society must respond to new challenges to ensure its own stability. Although it does not possess the same means of coercion as the totalitarian regimes of the 20th century, it does promote frenzied individualism while striving to enforce coexistence and a certain 'living-together' between people that come from *nowhere* and *everywhere*. It is a 'fluid' society in which cohesion is ensured by the propaganda apparatus; a total propaganda that affects all aspects of life, from the cradle to the grave; a global propaganda with multiple channels, including news, advertisements, films, series, video games, sports events, school curricula, publishing, official and community celebrations, and trainings; a global propaganda that reigns supreme over the world, or at least over the Western part of the world, with its successive 'epidemic' waves: Black Lives Matter, COVID, and the Russo-Ukrainian War. It is a violent sort of propaganda that stems from outside the social body and whose aim is not to consolidate traditional identities, but to fragment and erase them, while subordinating public opinion to the interests of minority lobbies — whether sexual, racial, religious, or simply financial and commercial. Because, as stated by Elon Musk, those 'who control the memes control the universe'. I, for one, call our contemporary Western society a propaganda society; a society where propaganda is widespread and proves to be the primary determinant that enables one to control social behaviour: a mental gulag imposed on us Europeans.

CHAPTER 1

TOTAL PROPAGANDA – WELCOME TO THE MENTAL GULAG

Global Propaganda

ONE OF THE GREAT rules of the press was, for a long time, that of proximity. Newspapers were thus interested in what was happening in the locations where their readers resided: in their towns, regions, and countries, but rarely beyond. In today's propaganda society, this rule has been upended. In successive waves, the media impose the same story about distant events that are scripted for all Western opinions. During the 1990s and 2000s, we witnessed the beginnings of Western opinion control with the first Gulf War of 1991, the war against Serbia in support of the Kosovo Albanians (1999), the September 11 attacks (2001), and Saddam Hussein's alleged 'weapons of mass destruction', which were used to justify the second Gulf War in 2004.

In the 2010s, the production pace characterising global propaganda campaigns accelerated further.

In 2015, the photo of little Aylan,[1] a boy found drowned on a Turkish beach, went viral in an attempt to make Europeans feel guilty and impose mass immigration on them. The result was 1.5 million illegal immigrants entering Germany in a single year, and now 400,000 non-European immigrants entering France annually.

In 2019, the death of African-American drug offender George Floyd, who was suffocated by a police officer in Minneapolis, dominated global news for several weeks. A routine police check gone wrong in a grim American suburb thus became a major global event. It also promoted the Black Lives Matter movement, establishing the notion that 'systemic White racism' actually existed, even though Black people, who represent 13.4% of the American population, actually commit 27% of all crimes and 37.4% of violent crimes in the United States. There are therefore two to three times more criminals within the African-American community than in the rest of the population. These facts, however, are simply impossible to point out in an atmosphere of media-related McCarthyism.

In the aftermath, the 2020 American election was featured in all Western media outlets, as if vassalised peoples could somehow participate in the choice of their American master. It was indeed a double-barrelled operation aiming to advance the existence of a US-centric Western consciousness while participating in the demonisation of populist opposition movements. The climax of this operation came about during the announcement of the results, with the good-natured commotion at the Capitol being presented as an attempted 'coup'.

Three months later, the COVID epidemic broke out. It was a twofold global pandemic: there was the disease itself, of course, but also the alarming news. The media opted for all the global data that was most likely to cause concern: the number of reported cases, the overcrowded hospitals, the number of deaths, while always choosing

---

1 TN: The boy's name was actually Alan Kurdi, with Aylan being the Turkish spelling. He and his brother drowned in the Mediterranean after their dinghy capsized in 2015.

the number — in absolute terms or in rates of progression — that was most likely to frighten people. Not to mention the emergence of new variants presented as ever more terrifying, if not in terms of their very lethality, then at least with regard to their contagiousness. The final figure was six million deaths worldwide in the space of two years, despite the fact that sixty million people die each year, thus representing 5% of all recorded deaths, as casualties generally occurred among the elderly or even the very elderly. In short, it was undoubtedly a concerning pulmonary disease but certainly not the great plague that we were led to believe as part of a global communications operation devised through the joint efforts of NGOs, consulting companies and Big Pharma.

With the arrival of the Omicron variant in the form of a more harmless flu, the discourse ('narrative in Frenglish')[2] surrounding COVID was running out of steam, and that is when the Russo-Ukrainian War broke out, bringing a new source of concern and fear. It was an event that generated a great deal of imagery: this time, the war (of aggression) was seen from the perspective of those targeted by the bombings and not from the cockpit of the bombers as was the case during the (just, obviously just) wars in Iraq and Serbia. It was an opportunity to set off a Disney-isation of international relations, with some good guys (Zelenskyy and the Ukrainians) and some bad guys (Putin and the Russians), all against a delirious backdrop of Godwin's law,[3] as Putin, the 'new Hitler', declared his intention to 'denazify' Ukraine. All of this was summed up by *Le Monde diplomatique*: 'A total event, an editorial crash'.

The globalisation of propaganda is also synonymous with the globalisation of the 'right number', i.e. the number that is most likely to arouse the greatest possible fear, or that of the most alarming events: tornadoes, droughts, floods, cold waves, heat waves, terrorist attacks,

---

2   TN: *Franglais* or 'Frenglish' refers to the tendency to overuse English words in the French language.

3   TN: According to Godwin's law, the longer an argument lasts, the greater the likelihood of someone (or something) being compared to Hitler.

serial murders, epidemics, pandemics, epizootics. Everything is covered!

It is thus hard not to regard this succession of media campaigns founded on powerful images and the arousing of fear as a far-reaching implementation of Naomi Klein's *Shock Doctrine* across all Western countries.

Tyrannical Propaganda: Altering Opinions

In traditional societies, propaganda was always limited: its sole function was to remind people about and reinforce the truths and values upheld by society. Such is the role of the priest's sermon (or the imam's): to call upon believers to respect the values and rules shared by the community, values from which it may be tempting to deviate individually.

As for contemporary propaganda, it is nothing of the sort. First of all, it does not limit itself to merely one hour a week… Secondly, its purpose is not so much to reinforce beliefs as to profoundly transform them and impose the values and interests of small minorities on a given majority. In this regard, one must refer to the Overton window, named after a conservative American lawyer and political scientist, that explained the range of political positions that can be expressed in public opinion: this framework shifts or, rather, is shifted by those who define the scope of permissible ideas. Thus, over the past three decades, unthinkable ideas have gradually become radical, then conceivable, acceptable, reasonable, popular, perhaps even obligatory, while ideas that were initially self-evident have gradually become questionable, disputable, and radical, if not extremist or even forbidden.

This massive global propaganda has fulfilled its main function of shifting the Overton window on many issues.

Same-sex marriage, for example, was once unthinkable. Today, opposing it means exposing oneself to the risk of being accused of homophobia, which constitutes a criminal offense in many countries.

OVERTON WINDOW

Unthinkable
Radical
Acceptable
Sensible
Popular
Policy
Popular
Sensible
Acceptable
Radical
Unthinkable

Abortion has long been heavily repressed; the Veil law legalised it in France under the notion of 'voluntary termination of pregnancy' (VTP) within certain restrictive conditions and up to the tenth week. Today, it has become difficult to challenge its legality up to the fourteenth week, despite the fact that the foetus's cranial bones must be broken at that stage for abortion to be performed. Abortion has even been made possible up to the end of the ninth month under the name of 'medical termination of pregnancy' (MTP), an MTP that is rather very similar to infanticide. New conventions, however, make this infanticide difficult to challenge. Meanwhile, those who attempt to offer distressed mothers alternatives to abortion run the risk of being prosecuted for obstruction. And global campaigns are regularly organised, particularly in an effort to exert pressure on American supreme courts, since the US is a country where pro-life movements are still active.

Long ago, freedom of expression was a cardinal value protected by the First Amendment to the American Constitution, the Declaration of Human Rights and the Charters of Freedom. This is no longer the case today, when the current watchword centres on the 'regulation' of people's freedom of expression, which is but a gentle euphemism for censorship. The platform-ic[4] TV talk show philosopher Raphaël Enthoven does not hesitate to describe the ideal of total freedom as 'liberticide', as its defenders find themselves accused. It is indeed true that if 'the Right wants freedom of expression, the Left wants freedom from oppression' (Grégory Roose[5]). And the question 'Is it true?' has gradually been replaced by the anxious question, 'Do we have the right to say it?'

In the wake of the Californian revolution of the 1960s and May 1968, one was, for a long time, 'forbidden to forbid', until the COVID epidemic made it possible to ban people from leaving their homes and accompanying a loved one on his/her great crossing into the realm of death, while also paving the way for the implementation of Chinese-style social control.

As part of a certain extension of the feminist #MeToo campaign, the presumption of innocence was abolished in favour of a requirement of suspicion. It is thus up to the accused to prove that they are not guilty of the past crimes with which they are being charged. Good luck with that!

Borders had long been a natural expression of sovereignty and their protection remained a state duty. Today, however, those who strive to protect their country from migratory invasion are demonised, their associations dissolved (the Identitarians in France), and their

---

4 TN: A play on words in reference to the term 'platonic'.

5 TN: Grégory Roose is a French short story writer and essayist who is also active as a columnist for a conservative French weekly.

members criminally prosecuted or even imprisoned for a time, as seen with the Englishman Tommy Robinson.

The death penalty had, likewise, long been considered to be an essential attribute of a sovereign state, but today, its mere persistence in a number of American states is regarded as an absolute horror. The idea of a world war, or even a nuclear one, once seemed like the ultimate disaster to be avoided: through successive escalations in the Russo-Ukrainian War, Western public opinion is now prepared to take such a risk, or at least to accept it.

These upheavals are indeed anything but spontaneous. Behind it all, there are active transnational forces serving certain very specific interests. The LGBTQ lobby was thus at the forefront of first imposing same-sex marriage, which was followed by assisted procreation without the presence of a father and then by surrogacy. The limitation of freedom of expression, particularly through the 'regulation' of social media at the hands of GAFA,[6] was conceived and planned during meetings of the Bilderberg Group and the Davos Forum, particularly in response to Trump's election in 2016. The demonisation of the borders and conservative regimes of Central Europe — Hungary and Poland — was orchestrated by pro-immigration associations and feminist lobbies funded by the European Union and numerous states, as well as by the Soros nebula. Big Pharma and major consulting firms (such as McKinsey) were instrumental in shaping public opinion around the world during the COVID-19 epidemic. Behind the rehabilitation of fresh and gleeful war are NATO's influence networks and the control they exert over a portion of Europe's political and media classes. Indeed, the 'military-intellectual lobby' (Pierre Conesa[7]) has not remained idle. The author of a remarkable essay entitled 'Tyranny

---

6   TN: Google, Apple, Facebook, and Amazon.

7   TN: Pierre Conesa is an expert on French foreign and internal politics, as well as on world military and political history.

Today', Philippe Bornet[8] studied the latter through the archetypes of Dionysius of Syracuse, Savonarola, Calvin, Robespierre, Billaud-Varenne, Stalin, and Mao Zedong. The essayist thus believes that tyranny can be recognised through the following signs: a predilection for the short term, bureaucracy, the control of information, hatred of both family and marriage, the indoctrination of children, a fascination with technology, population change, subjugation to foreigners, the introduction of an internal passport, and the use of religion or epidemics to consolidate power — all of which are characteristic of contemporary Western societies. In the absence of caves, stakes, guillotines and gulags to eliminate opponents, this has led our new tyrants to establish an unprecedented propaganda apparatus.

Mass Propaganda: 5% of the GDP or Even More?

At first glance, propaganda expenditures could be estimated at 2% of the gross domestic product of Western countries: indeed, 2% is the share of advertising expenditures in countries such as France. Advertising is not just mere 'publicity'; it presents various human models and, above all, promotes a certain kind of behaviour, namely that of a consumer. It even puts forward a human type: the *Homo consumens*, whose motto is 'I consume, therefore I am.' Advertising, therefore, shapes a given state of mind, similarly to the totalitarian regimes of the 20th century (the USSR, Nazi Germany) and the 21st (China, North Korea). Although the mindset is admittedly not identical, its shaping in the contemporary West is indeed comparable and undoubtedly more effective.

This 2% GDP estimate for the purposes of propaganda is, however, merely a default assessment. In actual fact, the media are not financed solely through advertising, but also participate in general indoctrination through their coverage of current events, their documentaries,

---

8 TN: Philippe Bornet is a senior lecturer at the Department of Slavic and South Asian Studies in Lausanne, Switzerland.

their reports, and the films and series that they screen. This applies, at the very least, to the mainstream media, i.e. the mass media, which attract 95% of all audiences, except in Hungary and Poland, where conservative media outlets fortunately compete with the progressive media, much to the chagrin of the Brussels authorities. And that's not all. The activities of many subsidised associations and 'NGOs', a high-sounding name used to promote the most politically correct outlets, mainly consist in agitprop activities: various operations, activist 'happenings', all of which are widely publicised by the media. There are even board games sold by large retailers, including *Antifa — The Game*.[9]

Far beyond the question of advertising expenditure, it is also important to consider the role of communications departments in government agencies, associations, and private companies when it comes to strategic decisions and official publications: the dominant line of these departments is 'not to rock the boat': they therefore act as watchdogs, constantly guiding institutional advertisements towards political correctness. And by submitting to it, they simply reinforce it, in harmony with a certain feedback process. Similarly, marketing rides the waves of the very trends of dominant propaganda, which it bolsters in turn. Any supermarket shelf is full of 'eco-responsible' or 'solidarity' products, in addition, of course, to the 'inclusive' ones. It's all about fostering people's 'living-together' and 'saving the planet', and nothing less than that: buying a yogurt thus becomes 'civic action' and choosing a carton of eggs a gesture of 'solidarity'.

It's a paradise that lies within reach, if not that of sinners, then at least that of buyers!

Likewise, the economy of generosity—involving associations and foundations that rely on donations—often relays the elements of dominant propaganda. Especially since corporate sponsorship has

---

9   TN: I actually had to check that this is real in order to believe it. It is indeed a very real board game sold in France, in which one plays the role of an antifascist group that fights against the far right.

become an instrument of their communications policy, allowing this type of expenditure to remain, in passing, exempt from taxation. In short, under the guise of generosity, large corporations create a positive image for themselves, at the expense of — you've guessed it — the taxpayer. Provided, of course, that the donation is geared towards promoting political correctness: the struggle against exclusion or global warming thus belongs to the hit parade of political correctness. Some companies venture even further: they get their customers to finance their generosity (!) by suggesting that they top up their purchases with a donation to one correct-thinking NGO or another. The kind-hearted customer of the French shoemaker Eram who buys shoes or clothing made in China is asked to fund Emmaüs[10] and, in the process, unwittingly encourages the foreign squatters of the Trotskyist association DAL.[11]

Lastly, the education provided by our National Education system and by various training organisations and businesses contains an ever-increasing amount of ideological bias.

As for the world of contemporary art, it is also subject to propaganda seizure.

It is difficult, however, to extract accurate statistics on the total domestic wealth dedicated to propaganda. Whatever the case, it is certainly more than 2% and probably more than 5% if we take into account the share of the media, their relevant associations and a portion of the budgets enjoyed by some companies' communications, training, and marketing departments. In the absence of precise figures, one is still not banned from reflecting on certain propaganda 'combos', including this little gem found in *The Huffington Post*:

---

10   TN: Emmaüs is an international solidarity movement founded in Paris in 1949 by Catholic priest and Capuchin friar Abbé Pierre in a desire to combat poverty and homelessness. It has now become secular.

11   TN: *Droit au logement* or the 'right to housing'.

In collaboration with *Le Slip Français*,[12] the solidarity association *La Fabrique nomade*, which works towards promoting the professional integration of refugee craftsmen and legalised migrants in France, has launched a collection of cotton voile bandanas and cotton canvas aprons, available for sale this Wednesday, October 13th. The collection is sponsored by designer Agnès B.

For the record, let us point out that Agnès B. defines herself as a 'committed' designer and that Le Slip français has SOS Racisme[13] provide training for its employees. One could easily laugh at this, mocking the bourgeois clientele that spends its money on underwear marketing, but that would be a mistake, because it is this very type of initiative that makes the ruling elites even more submissive to woke propaganda than the masses themselves.

From the Cradle to the Grave: Relentless Propaganda

The propaganda that the French and Europeans are subjected to is propaganda that permeates every moment of life and every hour of the day. 'You die, we do the rest' is a slogan used by some funeral homes. These services have undergone numerous developments with the emergence of 'funeral agreements' and 'funeral insurance'. The future deceased are encouraged to take precautions, no longer certain, in an increasingly individualistic society, that their children or loved ones will pay their last respects properly. This is yet another commodified activity, one that is therefore open to advertising propaganda.

More generally, older people are passive targets of propaganda, since they spend so much time in their armchairs, seated in front of the television screen, which spews forth propaganda as if from a tap. This is a source of tremendous political stability, with voter turnout

---

12   TN: Le Slip Français is an iconic French underwear and accessory brand.
13   TN: SOS Racisme is an international movement of anti-racist NGOs whose oldest chapter was established in France back in 1984.

remaining particularly high among older age groups. For pensioners, voting is like going to the post office: it remains a popular activity.

Propaganda, however, also affects younger people. Childcare centres and schools must be 'inclusive' and 'dismantle' racial and gender prejudice. The toy industry is under intense pressure to 'de-gender' its products. Dolls are now unisex, even transgender at times, displaying female faces with male attributes. Doll manufacturer Mattel is releasing a 'gay' version of Ken, Barbie's boyfriend. LEGO has, likewise, launched a series of 'queer' figurines. Children's book publishers are getting in on the act as well, with the inclusion of vegetarian wolves and of a gay, black Santa Claus.

Adults are, of course, no less immune to propaganda, primarily through their phone, tablet, and computer screens. This propaganda is all the more pervasive because the algorithms of major social networks prioritise political correctness and, through *shadow banning*, censor or render less visible all that does not abide by it. Not to mention television screens, which people keep willingly at home, but which are also imposed on them outside the home — in bars and restaurants, where TV channels pour forth their messages 24/7. It is no different with public transportation, where information screens provide travellers with insight that is certainly useful for the routes being taken, but punctuated with advertisements or propaganda messages. The threat of terrorism, endemic insecurity, epidemic risks, and even summer heatwaves multiply the opportunities to make announcements aimed at conditioning minds, often against a backdrop of fear. In France, the slightest TGV[14] journey thus exposes people to at least ten messages comprising Vigipirate[15] or COVID warnings: 'Any unattended baggage will be destroyed'; 'Failure to wear a face mask correctly can cost you 135€'; 'Protect yourself and protect others'; 'Stay hydrated!'; etc. Give us back our peace and quiet, damn it!

---

14   TN: High-speed train.
15   TN: Vigipirate is France's national security alert system relating to terrorism.

Cut off from nature yet obsessed with 'saving the planet', punitive ecology also offers ample material for the purpose of conditioning. School is *the* place where 'selective sorting' is learned, a sorting that must then be implemented throughout one's life. In this regard, northern countries have long been at the forefront of collective constraints and discipline. For their part, Latin countries, such as France, Spain, and Italy, have fallen in line with the German notion of *Ordnung*, which is but a source of ugliness in every landscape. Driving or simply using a car is now also increasingly regulated and discouraged; because we must all 'do our bit for the planet'.

Professional and Methodical Propaganda

Propaganda techniques were remarkably analysed in a *Que sais-je?*[16] penned by Christian-Democrat philosopher Jean-Marie Domenach. Based on his study of the functioning of the great totalitarian regimes of the 20th century (Hitler's Nazism and Stalinist Communism), as well as on various advertising methods, Jean-Marie Domenach defines five rules of propaganda that are rigorously applied by the oligarchy's media: simplification and the establishment of a single enemy; exaggeration and deformation; repetition and orchestration; transfusion; unanimity and contagion.

Simplification and the Establishment of a Single Enemy

The enemy of the oligarchy's media is clearly defined: any man that remains faithful to his ethnic, cultural, historical, and religious roots; all that is national, identity-based, patriotic, and Catholic; any person that is committed to certain anthropological continuities, traditional values, and his/her own homeland. The media thus present them with the following choice: to be labelled 'racist' or 'old-fashioned', or at best,

---

16 TN: Meaning 'What do I know?', a type of text that aims to clarify a certain topic.

'conservative'! The guilty party is accused of undermining accepted 'values': 'republican values' in the French version, and 'European values' in the Brussels version. As for these 'values', they boil down to the interpretation of various general texts in light of politically correct conformism at the hands of both judges and the media.

Exaggeration and Deformation

The positions espoused by the single enemy are distorted and caricatured. Such is the tyrannical condemnation of 'phobias': to criticise Islam is to be 'Islamophobic', to criticise gay propaganda 'homophobic', and not to believe that immigration is an advantage for host countries 'xenophobic'. Any politically incorrect speech is labelled as 'hate speech' and must be denounced and banned. It is the reign of accusatory inversion, of Newspeak, and of so-called 'decryptions' that are, in fact, nothing but conformist re-encryptions.

Repetition and Orchestration

The same news is broadcast everywhere, since many media outlets reiterate it and the source is often one and the same: the major Western news agencies, including Reuters, AP and AFP, are the sources of information that circulates in a loop across borders. 'The words are carefully weighed,' according to Ms. Léridon, the late AFP news director: 'weighed' in the scales of ideology and dominant interests, with beneficial or euphemistic vocabulary for some, and pejorative or demonising discourse for others.

One also encounters the same phrases everywhere: 'no amalgamation'; 'no stigmatisation'; 'Islam is a religion of peace'! The slogan itself serves as a thought. As for the bombings that target civilians, they are either serious 'war crimes' or limited 'collateral damage', depending on the perpetrators. Newspeak on every level!

We are, furthermore, faced with the same debaters racing from one media outlet to another, in a vast, closed circle. Not to mention, of course, the same 'experts'!

Transfusion

'Transfusion' is a propaganda technique that uses a popular idea to shift public opinion towards a different, even contradictory, point of view. Thus, the French *'Je suis Charlie'*[17] demonstration held on 11 January 2015 mobilised people around the topic of freedom of expression. The ensuing debate, however, focused instead on the limits to people's freedom of expression and the necessity to combat its abuses. We also encounter the struggle 'against hate speech', which serves as a smokescreen for the reduction of online freedoms and the undermining of media laws.

Unanimity and Contagion

Everyone must have the same thoughts simultaneously... It is the reign of echoic thinking and behavioural mimicry, which consist in posting the same opinions and banners on social media: Black Lives Matter at one time, the COVID-19 vaccine syringe at another, followed by the blue and yellow colours of the Ukrainian flag. Everyone, including celebrities, employers, artists or experts, sings the same tune to create an atmosphere of shock. Major ceremonies — the César Awards, Eurovision, Miss France, and sporting events — serve as pretexts for conditioning public opinion.

The same topic appears repeatedly at the same time. May 2022 was the time of the 'pregnant man': in advertising (Calvin Klein), with dolls, and in school exercises (life sciences). Smile — you're being assailed from all sides!

We live in an age of total propaganda imposed on everyone. There are no coincidences or amateurism in this regard: only force-feeding!

---

17 TN: The demonstration was organised in response to the slaughter of the staff at the *Charlie Hebdo* weekly at the hands of Islamists. The reason behind the massacre was the publication of caricatures depicting the prophet Muhammad.

Emotion and Shocking Images

As for shocking images, they are 'designed to disturb their recipients'. (Robert Redeker[18]). Some are displayed continuously, like the one of little Aylan or George Floyd. Others are, by contrast, forbidden, like the Bataclan[19] crime scene, which was censored on social media. In some cases, pity is obligatory, but in others, sensible anger is forbidden.

The Rainbow Ideology: Diversity Regime, Westernalism, Wokeism, and Progressivism

Behind the 'no-boat-rocking' attitude ('no balls, no hassle') lies the dominant ideology, which one kindly calls 'politically correct' or describes as 'one-track thinking', a real steamroller that denies all borders: between people, between the sexes, between territories and homelands.

This radical absence of borders has been labelled 'rainbow ideology' by essayist Martin Peltier. It is the rainbow of the LGBTQ lobby, promoting the rights of gay and trans minorities and displaying their multi-coloured flag in their parades. It is the rainbow of environmentalists, popularised by Greenpeace and the 'Rainbow Warriors'. It is the rainbow of the South African Republic, which is supposed to peacefully bring together the different races and ethnicities that constitute it.

As for Quebec political scientist Mathieu Bock-Côté, he popularised the expression 'diversity regime' wherever political balance is ensured by granting ever-increasing rights to various sexual, religious, ethnic and cultural minorities. Behind the 'living together' slogan hides the reality of 'living side by side': indeed, majority groups have given up on trying to have minorities accept a common legal system and forcing them to adapt to it.

---

18   TN: Robert Redeker is a French author and philosophy teacher.

19   TN: The Bataclan massacre was perpetrated by Muslim terrorists on 13 November 2015, as countless people were slaughtered during a concert. It was the deadliest attack in the EU since the Madrid train bombings of 2004.

Originating from North America as well, wokeism crossed the Atlantic in 2020 following the death of African-American drug offender George Floyd, who was suffocated during a police arrest. The advent of wokeism in Europe was not a given, though. The word itself means 'awakened' and describes African Americans who are aware of the oppression that they suffered during the era of legal segregation pervading the Southern states until the late 1960s. By extension, it nowadays applies to Black people who consider themselves victims of 'systemic White domination' and to repentant White people who adopt this point of view. European countries, which have not experienced the same situation as that of the United States (due to the limited presence of minorities or thanks to an assimilative outlook in both France and Portugal), were nevertheless quick to adopt the new American trend, despite, or perhaps because of, the violence of *cancel culture*: that is, the witch hunt consisting in the removal of statues, the renaming of squares and amphitheatres, and the denunciation of those who do not espouse correct thinking (*name and shame*).

This ideology is also Westernised: anything that happens in the United States—from presidential or midterm elections to miscellaneous news items—becomes a topic of both current events and propaganda to the European media. Whereas the traditional print media focused on local news, the mainstream media concentrate on what makes (ideological) sense, anywhere in the world. It is, in fact, the radical wing of the American Democratic Party that imposes such views, including the belligerent ones: any NATO war, or one that is at least supported by NATO, is inherently 'just' and leads to unequivocal war propaganda. This Westernism enjoys powerful GAFA (Big Tech) support, with these companies acting as both flagships of capitalism and as the economic and ideological extensions of the American *deep state* that nurtured them; all against a backdrop of global free trade.

With that said, the roots of the dominant ideology reach into a more distant past: that of the Enlightenment gone mad (Michel Geoffroy[20]),

---

20 TN: Michel Geoffroy is a French essayist and physician.

of limitless progressivism. It has a dual component: an individualistic one and a technological one. As for the techno-managerial component (increasingly restrictive procedures, increasingly frequent interfaces with robots), it is there to domesticate the individual. One readily mocks the reactionaries who believe that 'things were better before', yet no one derides the progressivists who believe that 'today is necessarily better than yesterday', because any new thing is considered inherently good. We must, however, rediscover critical thinking and assess the relevance of any change in terms of comfort, beauty, balance, conviviality, and fraternity. It is a question of both angle and point of view!

Thus multi-defined, the dominant ideology spreads its various myth-themes through propaganda: it is a free-trade, cosmopolitan, and globalist ideology advocating racial panmixis and miscegenation; the Benetton ideology of big capital which, thanks to the 'blessings' bestowed by the far Left, has become synonymous with creolisation; the notion of 'living together' thus becomes interchangeable with the cult of the Other, as Big Brother is used in the service of *Big Other* (Jean Raspail[21]). It is a world where the individual is king and enjoys new rights, such as same-sex marriage and the choice of one's gender identity, all while 'saving the planet' — a new categorical requirement — yet allowing real environmental problems to be obscured: it is 'the climate that hides the forest' (Guillaume Sainteny[22]). In short, the objective is neither man nor woman; neither Black nor White; neither Catholic nor Muslim; neither French nor German. It is, instead, what Renaud Camus[23] has termed UHM, i.e. undifferentiated human matter at the command of robots.

---

21   TN: Born in 1925, Jean Raspail was a French explorer, novelist, and travel writer.
22   TN: Guillaume Sainteny is an author that specialises in environmentalism and durable development.
23   TN: Renaud Camus is a French writer and novelist who coined the expression 'Great Replacement'.

CHAPTER II

TOTALITARIAN PROPAGANDA: THE GREAT ENTRAPMENT OF MINDS

Propaganda and Social Status

SOCIAL STATUS is based on distinction: the elites' game is to distinguish themselves from the masses through behaviour, style and opinions. At the same time, the people receive messages sent by the dominant ones and tend to conform to them in order to move closer to the elites. When a dominant person — an academic, a journalist, a scientist — develops progressive theories, he/she strengthens them while consolidating his/her social position. When a dominated person embraces them, they move closer to a dominant status.

Propaganda perpetuates itself through constant feedback: every time it strengthens itself, it is further strengthened through the interplay of censorship and self-censorship; the dominant opinion thus tends to become unique. Scholarly propaganda, popular propaganda, and institutional propaganda thus converge in a whirlwind of incessant global mimicry. Such is 'the contagion of indoctrination' presented by Konrad Lorenz[1] as one of the 'eight deadly sins of civilisation'.

Scholarly Propaganda

Science: A Sacrosanct Truth?

The authority argument is a powerful one. It's a well-known phenomenon in propaganda involving the transmission of knowledge or opinions from a 'knowledgeable' person to a layperson. Proponents of the *doxa*[2] like to rely on 'science' or, at the very least, on scientists, professors and experts. Such an attitude is, however, abusive: not all experts share the same point of view, but those that abide by the *doxa* are always the ones that are invited and re-invited to conferences and media shows. During the COVID-19 epidemic, the medical professors most present in the French media — including Karine Lacombe and Gilbert Deray — were those closest to the government and to pharmaceutical companies. The study published by the leading international medical journal *The Lancet* on the dangers of chloroquine[3] in the treatment of COVID-19 has been widely publicised in mainstream media, even though it only took a few minutes of analysis to realise that it was based on bogus data. The climate experts that are regularly invited are also those that promote the most alarmist models.

Naively, the public believes that science is 'neutral', which is a mistake: indeed, rivalries are fierce in an effort to obtain research funding, promotions or awards, international titles, publisher support, and access to the media, which in turn determines the obtainment of funding and editorial opportunities. A physicist, a former expert at the IPCC,[4]

---

1 TN: Konrad Zacharias Lorenz was an Austrian zoologist, ethologist, and ornithologist who won the 1973 Nobel Prize in Physiology or Medicine along with Nikolaas Tinbergen and Karl von Frisch.
2 Editor's note: Greek: 'popular opinion'.
3 TN: Chloroquine belongs to a group of medicines used to treat malaria.
4 TN: The Intergovernmental Panel on Climate Change.

and the author of a climate-realistic book entitled *L'urgence climatique est un leurre*,[5] François Gervais has explained that he would advise any young researcher eager to make a career for himself not to opt for a thesis topic that is likely to challenge or temper the theory of the anthropogenic origin of global warming or even the latter's catastrophic nature.

History is also the focus of constant ideological manipulation: Muslim Spain (*Al-Andalus* or Andalusia) is described as a paradise of 'living together', while the Spanish Civil War is rekindled and re-written 85 years after coming to an end. In France, it is the American historian Paxton who holds the official truth about the Vichy regime, and only his followers are invited to speak about it. For his part, Benjamin Stora has an absolute monopoly over the history of Algeria.

Statistics: Concealment and Confusion

'There are three kinds of lies: lies, damned lies, and statistics', as Winston Churchill is said to have stated.[6] The first statistical manipulation relates to the choice of what to study and what not, as well as to deciding which correlations to establish and what raw data to make public or ignore. Thus, when analysing COVID-related deaths, one has witnessed much greater polarisation in connection with people's 'vaccination status' than in relation to people's co-morbidities or their undergoing treatment or not.

The questions asked (and those that are not), however, determine the answers. For instance, I once questioned a professor of quantitative geography regarding the impact of the immigrant presence on housing prices in a given neighbourhood. His answer was clear and unequivocal: 'There are no such studies; it is an exceedingly touchy

---

5   TN: Climatic Urgency Is a Delusion.
6   TN: This seems to be untrue, as the statement was, in fact, once attributed to Mark Twain, who then attributed it to British Prime Minister Benjamin Disraeli (1804–1881).

matter.' Michèle Tribalat, a demographer at the INED (the National Institute of Demographic Studies), thus titled one of her books: '*Les Yeux grands fermés — L'immigration en France*',[7] accusing Hervé Le Bras, one of the leading thinkers or rather ready-made thinkers of French demographics, of 'statistical genocide'. Another media star, this Le Bras chap! Indeed, he popularised the notion of 'net migration', a statistical manipulation that allows the number of foreigners entering France to be subtracted from the number of French people who *leave*. Nice three-card trick! Apart from Great Britain and some Scandinavian countries, it is difficult in Europe to have knowledge, especially recent knowledge, of academic success, unemployment rates, and crime figures based on people's ethnic origin. In Germany, the former SPD (Social Democratic Party) public figure, Thilo Sarrazin, has been the focus of public condemnation since daring to reveal but a part of the dangers of Muslim immigration.

Polls: The Opinion Factory

Polls surfaced with the emergence of public relations campaigns in the United States — to determine consumer opinion and to influence it.

Three effects must thus be taken into account here:

- The bias of the question itself, which can encourage responses in one direction rather than another;
- The evolution of responses over time, which assesses the effect of opinion campaigns according to the following principle: you ask a question; you campaign on the subject; you ask the question again; you determine the change; you publicise it openly; you ask the question again, thereby triggering a cascade effect;
- The self-fulfilling and particularly well-documented prophecy in electoral terms: any candidates promoted by the media are advantaged in polls, and this advantage gradually becomes an electoral

---

7 TN: Immigration in France: Eyes Wide Shut.

reality, which *retrospectively* reinforces the predictive nature of polling.

The World of Publishing: Serving What Is 'Good'

Since the days of Gutenberg, the world of books had long been a struggle for freedom, but this is no longer the case. At all the major book fairs, whether in Frankfurt, Paris or Montreuil for the youth sector, the thought police keep watch, sometimes assisted by the 'antifa', those violent far-left militias who hunt down 'intruders'. Publishers — at least the major ones, i.e. those whose books are everywhere — have thus become remarkable advocates of conformist opinion, and especially of censorship. The mechanism is as follows. Their primary customers belong to the intellectual class, not only those who read but particularly those who instruct or give instructions (booksellers, librarians, professors). It is an environment in which left-wing culture is dominant and accompanied by sectarianism: they don't just promote what is 'good', but also ostracise the 'bad'. Such is the first bias.

The sale of a book also depends on its advertising in catalogues and its availability on the shelves of bookstores (or even supermarkets). However, what determines this distribution is media coverage, which is itself conditioned by conformity. The communications departments of major publishers are therefore very careful to promote political correctness, which acts as a guarantee of obtaining proper media coverage; just as they are vigilant in their hunt for 'black sheep', whose presence is likely to result in a bad image for the publishing house. And that is the second bias. Even the authors themselves participate in this witch hunt by refusing to be published alongside colleagues or peers whose thinking is deemed unacceptable. Such is the third bias. The circle is thus complete. Renaud Camus, expelled from Fayard, and Richard Millet, excluded by Gallimard, could attest to this.

Writers thus quickly understand that their talent can only be recognised if they establish their credentials and write with a rainbow keyboard. Worse still: university professors, whose very status guarantees their independence, take into account the commercial and convenience concerns of their publishers in the choice and orientation of their research, which creates a truly liberticidal network.

Artistic Warfare: Deconstruction in Progress

The world of culture is diverse. There are defenders of heritage, who, by nature, are rather conservative, and followers of 'hidden art' (Aude de Kerros[8]), who use traditional disciplines (painting, sculpture, engraving, bookbinding) in their quest for beauty, drawing inspiration from Europe's long legacy. This is not, however, the case with official art, an art form subsidised by public authorities or major patrons of the arts. This 'conceptual art' has been imposing its presence from Helsinki to Venice, from Bilbao to Vienna. The kitschy sculptures of Jeff Koons or the works of 'visual artist' Anish Kapoor are making their way into the palace and park of Versailles. With a triple aim: firstly, an ideological one, namely that of desecrating and dismantling Europe's most significant sites; next, a speculative one, as exhibitions in prestigious sites give 'value' to the works; last but not least, the purpose is to amaze and intimidate public opinion: the *vulgum pecus* is called upon to bow down, because daring to doubt would mean demoting oneself. It is an imperative of conformity to which the elites are particularly sensitive.

The Mass Media – The Hub of the 'Good Camp'

The mainstream media operate in accordance with the big capital alliance (i.e. the oligarchs who own them) and that of the journalists who contribute to it all. Save for some rare exceptions, these forces synergise and converge towards liberal-libertarian ideology and the promotion

---

8   TN: Born in Jakarta in 1947, Aude de Kerros is a French painter, sculptor, art critic, and essayist.

of the 'nomadic world' (Attali[9]) in the face of entrenchment. The media play a dual role in the dissemination of progressive propaganda: they are the key to allowing the elites (scientists; academics; literary, artistic, economic and political figures) to access public visibility, which is, in itself, a prerequisite for career advancement. Pleasing the media is therefore a near-obligation — in terms of form, of course, but also in terms of content. At the same time, the media contribute to shaping the opinions of the elites through the ideas that they promote, while also pushing to reduce cognitive dissonance among those who want to access their content: if you want to express an opinion out of sheer opportunism, it quickly becomes more comfortable to adopt the right one as your own or, at the very least, to water down the one you have.

GAFA: Censorship at the Click of a Keyboard

The internet had long provided free access to information that evades ideological and political conformity. Brexit and Trump's election in 2016, however, led people to question the principle of online neutrality.

The Davos Forum and the Bilderberg Group have both addressed the issue of the 'necessary regulation' of the internet. In the wake of this development, major social networks undertook a threefold action:

- That of validating 'accurate information' in collaboration with mainstream media;
- That of modifying algorithms in favour of 'good' information;
- That of censoring fake news and sometimes blatantly false information, but, more often than not, any unpleasant information too (regarding the Great Replacement, COVID-19, health policies, criminality, elections, etc.). Media fact-checkers are often nothing more than fact-*chekists* that act as a thought police: just like the

---

9   TN: In addition to being an author, a political advisor and a senior civil servant, 81-year-old Jacques José Mardoché Attali is a French economic and social theorist who has published 86 books in 54 years, between 1969 and 2023.

Cheka, the political police of the new Bolshevik regime in 1917. GAFA thus plays a major role in this regard by providing the lies of propaganda with immunity. However, the media and GAFA also act as a bridge between those who hold ideological power and the people that they feed through their televisions, phones, and computer screens — which brings us to the topic of popular propaganda.

Popular Propaganda

Advertising: Honour to Whom Honour Is Due

Advertising is at the heart of the capitalist world. It is a key element of competition between brands, products, categories of goods, and distribution methods (small businesses, large retail outlets, online purchases).

Advertising is not, however, neutral: indeed, it monopolises the 'available brain time' (Le Lay) of those who experience it, guiding it in one single direction: towards the act of purchasing, all to the detriment of the time that could be devoted to other free activities, such as reading, tending to one's garden, walking in the forest, tinkering, exercising, taking care of one's children, visiting one's parents, meeting friends, and playing board games. Advertising aims to steer our lives in one single direction: that of consumption!

Advertising influences our lifestyles: it was the vector for the establishment of the American way of life in Europe, thanks to the comfort afforded by the abundance of manufactured products, such as over-processed foods and sodas. It is at the root of the spread of 'globesia', the obesity epidemic that affects the entire Western world and perhaps even the whole world. It accelerates the replacement of classical French words with Anglo-Saxon gibberish.

In actual fact, advertising not only impacts, but even creates lifestyles: the materialism of the 1960s has thus been replaced by the *Homo festivus* of the 2000s.

Likewise, advertising makes use of the mechanisms of social distinction and channels the latter into a trendy ideological approach: the notion of 'organic' food and the energy transition in people's choice of housing or cars (hybrid ones, of course…) have thus become the driving forces of both the market and opinion change. Protecting the 'planet' now serves as a sales argument and as a means to increase profit. Such is 'green (and therefore "virtuous") growth'.

Advertising goes even further, promoting human types derived from 'diversity' and the Great Replacement. In France, President Macron estimates that 'the number of fellow citizens with family on the southern shore of the Mediterranean' totals ten million, i.e. around 15% of the population. In the advertisements of major companies, however, men and women of North African or sub-Saharan descent actually represent 30%. This overemphasis can only be accounted for by ideological, and not commercial, reasons. Even more surprising is the fact that a third of the couples depicted are ethnically mixed. It is thus hard not to perceive this statistical anomaly as a message in favour of a type of mixed race, most often involving a Black (or Arabian) man with a White, European woman. It is but another element serving the interests of a woke ideology that demeans the heterosexual European man.

The impact of advertising on public opinion is considerable for three reasons:

- First of all, advertising reaches the entire population.
- However, it primarily targets children, who, in the eyes of advertisers, offer three advantages: a message aimed at a minor costs three times less than one aimed at an adult; and its effectiveness is greater because when a child is attracted to a product or a brand they are potentially attracted to it for life; last but not least, children

often act as influencers on their parents. The appeal of children to advertisers is therefore so significant that some analysts have been speaking of 'advertising pedophilia'.

- High-income groups and elites are another priority target of advertising, as they consume more due to their higher incomes. And, above all, they devote the latter to high value-added products that offer high margins to producers while also requiring higher advertising costs: advertising accounts for more of the cost price of a Porsche Panamera than that of a Fiat Panda, and more in the case of a Montblanc pen than a Bic's. Lastly, wealthy social classes are subject to advertising investments that are all higher because their choices are subsequently emulated: if we take the automobile industry, for instance, the upper socio-professional classes were the first to drive market trends, with cars that were faster, then more comfortable, then safer, and now more environmentally friendly (or at least deemed so). One thus bears witness to a major phenomenon: upper classes precede the general public while being subjected to conformist pressure more than anyone else.

Literature: From the Nobel Prize to Crime Novels

Literature has always been and remains a pivotal point in the cultural struggle, and a genuine network is being established today, stretching from the Nobel Prize to crime novels. In 2021, an unknown Tanzanian author was thus awarded the prize by the Stockholm Academy. Abdulrazak Gurnah's sole merit was him being African and having published around ten books in London, in which, according to the BBC, 'he explores the impact of colonialism on East African identity and the experience of refugees who are forced to find a home elsewhere.'

As regards comfort literature, the trend now leans towards Nordic thrillers that combine icy exoticism with humanitarian conformity, narrating the joys and sorrows of a Syrian refugee or those of a lonely Afghan minor. Such consumer products are now widespread throughout Europe. The Swiss are not to be outdone: in *The Dragon of Muveran*, a police officer involved in a same-sex relationship hunts a serial killer across the limestone mountains of the Vaud canton, a serial killer who turns out to be a conservative female pastor.

The great classics are not immune to sanitising either: Agatha Christie's *Ten Little Niggers* has thus been renamed *And Then There Were None*. And as for Joseph Conrad's novel *The Nigger of the 'Narcissus'*, a title deemed 'offensive', it has been re-baptised as *The Children of the Sea*. Worthy of an Orwellian novel! Not even comics lag behind: Ken Kent, the son of Superman, 'falls in love with a man and embraces his bisexual identity', declares the publisher DC Comics, a subsidiary of Warner Bros.

Children's literature is also undergoing normalisation. In France itself, the charter for young writers — which governs their involvement in schools and associations (their main source of income) — requires them to adopt a civic-minded approach and demonstrate allegiance to the struggle against discrimination. The rules of the now-defunct Union of Soviet Writers are very much alive.

Hollywood: Conquering Minds to Conquer Markets

As early as 1945, the Americans took advantage of their presence in Europe to impose the opening of cultural markets. In the tradition of Bernays' *Propaganda*, they chose to ensnare minds so as to spread their way of life and conquer markets. And it is Hollywood that has served the purposes of American imperialism: war-related imperialism (*The Longest Day*, *Saving Private Ryan*), and commercial imperialism (Product investment! Coca-Cola forever…), now followed by woke imperialism. On 22 May 2013, Joe Biden, who, at the time, acted as Barack Obama's vice president, did not hesitate to state that it was the Hollywood industry that had 'helped to change people's attitudes on same-sex marriage'. And in the final instalment of the Bond film series, James Bond retires, as the 007 badge is handed to a young black woman. There's indeed *No Time to Die*, but always enough for the Great Replacement! Not even history is immune to re-writing. Although concerned with historical accuracy, Ridley Scott was forced to include Black soldiers in his *Napoleon* in order to secure funding for his next film. As for fairy tales, they are also rather exploited: Disney's new *Cinderella* is thus a young trouser-wearing businesswoman, while the fairy godmother is a black actor playing the part of a gay man. In his *Patrouille du conte*,[10] Pierre Gripari[11] had depicted a patrol comprised of eight children, led by a lieutenant and managed by a captain, tasked with policing the kingdom of fairy tales. That was in 1982. Forty years later, reality has actually caught up with fiction.

The Dream (or Nightmare) World of Television Series

The cinematic domain is steadily losing ground in favour of television series, which are also becoming increasingly disconnected from tradition and reality. A successful writer of children's books was thus approached by a major television station to write the script for a heroic fantasy series set in a Gallic village. When he submitted a first draft, the synopsis was applauded but criticised for lacking 'diversity'. Making use of a little imagination, the author then invented a hero of African origin, much to the contentment of the client, who then asked him to also include a homosexual character. Realising that he would not be able to cope with such increasingly burdensome demands, the writer gave up any desire to put his talent at the service of the rainbow cause and abandoned the lucrative contract and the fame that would have resulted from it all. This, however, is merely the exception that

---

10   TN: (Fairy) Tale Patrol.
11   TN: Gripari was a French writer who openly acknowledged his own homosexuality.

confirms the rule, as the majority of writers and directors anticipate the constraints of political correctness. For eighteen years, the French were conditioned by *Plus belle la vie*[12] on France 3:[13] in a friendly and jovial Marseille setting. Genre scenes were aplenty, including an assault perpetrated by a gang of White thugs against a kind North African man, all because of a cigarette. One is immediately reminded of Jean Gabin's [14]line in *The President*: 'There are flying fish, but they are not representative of the species'. On France 2, *Un si beau soleil*[15] conveys—this time in a Languedoc setting—the image of a France that is racially mixed and open to all societal developments. These sugary French soap operas are, however, nothing compared to the great machines embodied by Amazon and Disney. For these entertainment-propaganda giants it's all about updating the image of great literature and cinematic works. Revisited in this way, *The Lord of the Rings* series is the polar opposite of Tolkien's great European mythological work and its admirable cinematic adaptation in Peter Jackson's trilogy. As for George Lucas's cult series *Star Wars*, it simply had to be re-done in light of the LGBT revolution. And Disney+ has just released, with resounding fanfare, a series about Malik Oussekine, a French precursor to George Floyd. Oussekine was a far-left, diabetic North African protester who died in 1986 (!) after being beaten by police officers that belonged to a police motorcycle unit. For the proponents of wokeism, there is clearly neither forgiving nor forgetting!

---

12 TN: *A More Beautiful Life*, a French television soap opera/drama series based on an idea by Hubert Besson and characters created by Georges Desmouceaux.
13 TN: France 3 is a French free-to-air public television regional network that belongs to the France Télévisions group.
14 TN: Jean Gabin was a famous French actor and singer.
15 TN: Such a Beautiful Sun.

The Eighth Art of Video Games Is Not Immune!

If cinema is indeed the seventh art form,[16] then video games could well be the eighth. In terms of jobs, the domain is a paradise for computer scientists, graphic designers, and art designers. This cultural industry's turnover is equivalent to that of the cinematic industry and popular arts combined. Some games have even managed to gross six billion dollars, which is twice as much as *Avatar*, the greatest commercial success in cinematic history. Propagandists cannot, therefore, afford to ignore a universe that appeals to children (boys in particular), teenagers, young adults, and even older people… Especially since the major cultural machines — Disney, Amazon, and Microsoft — have made substantial investments in this sector.

Some American war video games are like American films: epic, violent, and very patriotic (with their army taking pride of place!). Many games also emphasise the 'racialisation' of their characters, which is understandable in the case of *LEGO Star Wars*, since the original game has been multiracial from the outset, but less easy to justify in the case of *Battlefield 1*, whose theme centres on World War I: in the fiction, black people are very present indeed, whereas in reality, colonial troops did not intervene on the German side at all and represented a mere 4% of the French troops. The *Assassin's Creed* series, which focuses on detective investigations through time, also spreads disinformation when depicting black people in ancient Greece or the Middle Ages!

With that said, video games are not the most favourable (game) field for woke propaganda: firstly, because many entertainment themes fall into the heroic fantasy category, which relates a heroic story within a fantastical world; secondly, because a significant part of the activity itself consists in more or less ritualised combat and rarely in the spirit

---

16   TN: In French culture, cinema is known as the seventh art because it combines elements of the first six, namely architecture, sculpture, painting, music, dance, and literature, which results in a new form of artistic expression.

of 'togetherness'; thirdly, because the Japanese, whether directly or through the *manga* mindset, exert great influence on the sector and remain relatively unaffected by wokeism; and last but not least, because players enjoy a certain autonomy in their game purchases and their choice of characters and accessories. Therefore, not all manipulations are equally possible. For example, *Cyberpunk 2077* may offer players the option of customising their character as a transgender one (a man with a vagina and pink hair), but it cannot force them to do so, nor can it prevent the issue from sparking raging online controversy.

Reality TV: Subtle Conditioning

Reality TV shows that cast 'real people' in (more or less) real roles also serve the purpose of subtle conditioning. The M6[17] channel stands out with *Chasseurs d'appart* and *Maison à vendre*.[18] The shows are headed by a prominent real estate agent, Stéphane Plaza, who also has a career as a theatre and television series actor. The 'cast' itself is representative — without any obvious bias — of the French reality of home buyers and sellers: singles, couples, small families, retirees; as for same-sex or 'mixed' couples, they are rather rare. Identifying with real people is thus bound to be strong. The influence is nonetheless significant when it comes to serving the interests of fashion normalisation and the devaluation of the old in favour of the new. In line with a progressive society, in which any tomorrow is necessarily better than any yesterday, one must break down barriers and redecorate. The old is, by its very nature, outdated and not 'vintage'. The kitchen must thus be open-plan and have a lunch counter, and the main room must comprise a master bedroom with a bathroom. Although the show undoubtedly follows the logic of societal evolution towards ever-increasing comfort and

---

17   TN: Also known as Métropole Television, M6 is the most profitable private national French television channel and the third most watched television network in French-speaking countries.

18   TN: Flat Hunters and House for Sale.

individualism, it also reinforces the latter by making it a categorical imperative. Furthermore, the show takes great care to ignore certain essential selection criteria: the distance of a suggested property from the city centre is indeed discussed, but never the issues of safety, neighbours, quality and school attendance. These are extremely crucial aspects for buyers to consider, but since they relate to immigration issues, they remain taboo.

Popular Art — Stupefying and Astounding

Through its fans and success, pop music plays an important role in transmitting values, codes, behaviours, and aesthetics to those that listen to it. From this perspective, it is significant to realise that one of the most popular music genres in Europe, one that half of all young people in France listen to, is RAP (Rock against Police).[19] A musical genre born in Black American ghettos, it involves African rhythms, staccato speech, and often a hatred of Whites. This musical genre spread throughout Europe, and particularly to Spain, in the vicinity of American military bases inhabited by African Americans. France, for its part, is home to the second largest rap scene in the world, which is particularly due to the strong African presence in our country, as well as to the powerful support offered by production companies and media outlets: Skyrock, which acts as a radio station for advertising, and Mouv'[20] in terms of public 'utility' (?).

The Eurovision contest, which some call 'Americanovision', also plays a role in spreading the phenomenon. For obvious political reasons, it was Ukraine that won the competition in 2022, but not without first incorporating the necessary dose of rap into traditional music presented in an electronic music version: talk about the art of putting

---

19   TN: To my knowledge, the word 'rap' has nothing to do with Rock Music; nor is it an acronym of any kind.

20   TN: Formerly known as Le Mouv', Mouv' is a French youth-oriented radio station launched in 1997.

nationalism at the service of wokeism! The hijacking of Eurovision to serve the dominant ideology is constant: we have thus witnessed an increasingly frequent use of the Anglo-American language, blatantly geopolitical choices (Ukraine's victory in 2015 and 2022, Russia's exclusion in 2016), 'committed' lyrics, and the 2014 victory of Conchita Wurst, the Austrian bearded woman.

And as might be expected, the major international film festivals — the Oscars in Hollywood, the César Awards in Cannes — act in unison: the juries, nominations, and award winners are thus selected based on political correctness and, henceforth, wokeism.

Beauty pageants have also been hijacked. Initially, the Miss France pageant was a good-humoured spectacle that consisted in choosing the most beautiful young woman once the contestants had paraded in formal dresses and swimsuits. Quite innocent, one might say. Indeed, too innocent for the deconstructionist ideologists who then decided to 'embellish' (?) the parade by focusing on more serious issues than a woman's appearance and measurements, such as her origins, education, and ambitions, within a framework akin to that of motivational letters, that of the fight against racism, or one's involvement in humanitarian work, all of which allow participants to be awarded points by the jury, and even by the public! Likewise, 'diversity' has made its entrance into the competition: what could be more normal than a beautiful mixed-race woman competing as Miss Guadeloupe or Miss Martinique? But a Miss Alsace or Miss Limousin? Forget it. As if this were not enough, the Miss France 2022 competition will be open to transsexuals, i.e. to men (at least chromosome-wise).

Sports — The Opium of the People

When, in 1894, Baron Pierre de Coubertin restored the Olympic Games in accordance with the spirit of antiquity, he dreamt of keeping the influence of money and politics at bay. It was a gamble that would fail. It was indeed irenic, as Greek cities continued to organise such events in their stadiums...[21] Politics thus quickly became inseparable from the confrontations between athletes. Admirably filmed by Leni Riefenstahl, the Berlin Games of 1936 were a gem of image-based propaganda. The post-Second World War period was no exception: after Black Americans had raised Black Power fists on the podium of the 1968 Mexico City Games, and the Palestinian attack in Munich in 1972, came the takeover conducted by *big businesses* and Coca-Cola in Atlanta, 1996. In the eyes of Robert Redeker, this 'global mercantile spectacle' serves a dual purpose: the domestication of the body and that of the soul.

More than the Olympic Games, however, it is actually ball games, and particularly football, that are at the heart of contemporary propaganda. 'It is the High Mass of planetary uprooting: one that serves to strengthen cosmopolitan faith,' says Michel Geoffroy. The FIFA World Cup once witnessed national teams compete against one another in a patriotic contest. Nowadays, however, the World Cup showcases multi-racial and multi-religious mercenary teams and drives people to identify with players who look nothing like them. In this area, France has been a pioneering country: open to excessive immigration before other European countries and steeped in universalist values, it promoted integration through football. The 1998 World Cup victory was presented as that of a 'Black-White-Arab' team. The Germans, the Spanish, the Italians, and the British have since adopted the same model. More recently, and in contrast with the utopian vision of assimilation, football has been used to relay the propaganda of the Black Lives Matter movement, forcing players to kneel in front of billions of spectators and viewers. Football is also a formidable machine for promoting market values and social inequality: low-wage workers thus identify with stars that earn more in a single year than they could hope to accumulate in 3,000 lives, idolising them.

---

21 TN: The first modern Olympic Games took place in Athens in 1896.

Since propaganda never rests, a new front has just been opened—that of transsexuals: it is the new craze of the 2020s, allowing men who declare themselves women to participate in and win competitions against opponents whose very biology—namely their pair of XX chromosomes—has not endowed them with the same muscular advantages.

> If I had ever had doubts about the political nature of sports, a certain anecdote would definitively have opened my eyes. In 2004, during a career dispute with the hierarchy of our Ministry of the Interior, a (good) colleague of mine explained to me that he couldn't support me because I had 'failed in my duty of discretion'. When I asked him what he meant, he replied: 'You criticised the French football team.' Indeed, in an effort to dispel the propaganda, I had (astutely) pointed out in 2002 that the French Black-White-Arab team had been eliminated by the eleven blond Vikings of Denmark! This was seen as almost a crime of *lèse-majesté*.[22]

Institution-Based Propaganda

Schools: Indoctrination Rather than Education

In almost all European countries, but in France more than anywhere else, academic performances (as measured by PISA[23] studies) are plummeting, which is true of young people's levels of proficiency in languages and their mastery of mathematics, physics, and history (and even their athletic abilities). However, it would be a mistake to see this as a failure of our European education systems. Quite to the contrary, the prevailing educational programmes and methods are part of a deconstructionist approach:

- They break the chain of knowledge transmission;
- They instil historical guilt;

---

22 TN: The author does not specify who has made this statement.
23 TN: Programme for International Student Assessment.

- They cast doubt upon people's ethnic, sexual, cultural, and civilisational identities;
- They undermine the very foundations that enable the development of critical thinking;
- They impose a certain 'presentist' system, encouraging commentary on current events through what the media claim;
- They saturate young minds with ideological conformity: with 'anti-racism', repentance, gender equality, the protection of sexual minorities, and nowadays also 'transgenderism'.

By declaring in his inauguration speech of May 2022 that he wanted 'an ever more inclusive school system, providing fundamental knowledge and forging republican mindsets', President Macron let the cat out of the bag. Indeed, his plan for young people's education is primarily ideological, which he confirmed by appointing wokeist Pap Ndiaye as Minister of Education.

Let these gentlemen rest assured, however: our schools perform poorly in terms of education, but they do indoctrinate well! Such is the Order of the S(ch)olar Temple, and not just in France. In both our national and European elections, first-time voters (aged eighteen to twenty-four) are more likely to vote for 'progressive' parties than other age groups. And far-left militias recruit their members primarily amongst high school and university students, just as they constitute the bulk of Greta Thunberg's fan base, worshipping the prophetess of catastrophic ecology and serving as the cannon fodder for Extinction Rebellion,[24] the horsemen of the Apocalypse that Soros has unleashed upon Europe.

---

24 TN: Sometimes abbreviated as XR, Extinction Rebellion is a UK-based global environmental movement whose declared aim is one of using non-violent civil disobedience to push governments towards intervention regarding climatic issues, the loss of biodiversity, and the threat of social and ecological collapse.

Official Communication: Daily Conditioning

Official communication is now running at full speed. Although Catholic holidays and Mother's Day are threatened with disappearance, commemorative days are actually multiplying and are increasingly exploited for propaganda purposes: one thus commemorates the deportation of the Jews, the Holocaust, slavery, colonisation, International Women's Day, gender equality, and people's disabilities, and there is even a car-free day to celebrate. The list goes on and on. And as if this weren't enough, there are now weeks, months, and years being devoted to this litany of endless propaganda.

The European Union is at the forefront of this game: in 2019, the 'Young European of the Year' was a veiled Turkish woman waving the European flag in Rome, in front of the Colosseum. In 2022, on the occasion of the 'European Year of Youth', it was another veiled young woman that spoke in front of the camera. Was there a difference? Yes, because in 2022, the veil covered even more of her body!

At the same time, in France, the Ministry of Public Health launched a powerful poster campaign with the following slogans: 'Yes, my daughter is a lesbian'; 'Yes, my roommate is a lesbian'; 'Yes, my father is gay'; 'Yes, my friend is gay'; 'Yes, my granddaughter is trans'. You get the idea: heterosexuality is no longer in vogue. It is thus difficult not to perceive this as the very stranglehold of the Great Replacement: bestowing value upon others while discouraging Europeans from perpetuating themselves. Germany is even more at the forefront, going as far as to conduct voluntary sterilisation campaigns for women on public television.

History is also being exploited. In 2016, the French government attempted to impose the presence of rapper Black M to commemorate the centenary of the Battle of Verdun. Faced with the outcry, it contented itself with Les Tambours du Bronx,[25] who provided the

---

25 TN: The band plays a percussion-based combination of industrial music, afrobeat, drum and bass, hip hop, rock, metal, hardcore, and techno.

rhythm for the deliberately disorderly surge of 3,400 young French and German people dressed in colourful T-shirts, amidst the graves of the Douaumont ossuary.

This official conditioning does not end there, however. It also strives to seize control of everyday behaviour: on our roads, first of all, with awareness messages and automated electronic checkpoints; next, when it comes to recycling, which is necessarily selective: having long been at the forefront of this taming (under the pretext of safeguarding the environment), Germany and the Nordic countries are now being overtaken by Latin ones. Last but not least, the COVID-19 crisis enabled a new advancement in the society of propaganda and control. Under the guise of 'prevention', Europe has become the great Western hospital, where 'every healthy person is an ill individual unaware of his illness' (*Dr Knock* by Jules Romains[26]). Such is the *Big Mother* State.

A Totalitarian Enterprise

Companies had long been a place of political neutrality. Their purpose was to remunerate their shareholders through profit and their employees through salaries, all under the authority of a far-sighted sort of management and with absolute respect for the opinions of customers, suppliers, shareholders, and employees. This, however, is no longer the case.

Indeed, companies are now establishing 'ethics committees' and 'values charters', similar to the famous 'republican values' or 'European values' promoted by our media and politicians. In fact, the word 'values' is an umbrella term, a Newspeak word meaning 'in line with political correctness', i.e. striving for 'sustainable development', 'diversity', social and racial mixing, and the introduction of a ban on reality. Rating agencies are doing their bit too by conducting ESG assessments of large companies: E is for the environment, S for what is social and societal, and G for governance. To fully understand the graveness of

---

26 TN: Jules Romains was a French poet and author.

this nonsense, one should note that the multinationals involved in elder abuse—KORIAN, ORPEA—received excellent scores! Well done! It was, in fact, Elon Musk who best defined the ESG score: 'It depends on your company's compatibility with the leftist agenda.'

Businesses are actually places that shape minds through advertising propaganda that isn't merely 'promotional', but extols certain lifestyles and promotes the Great Replacement, racial mixing, and the glorification of homosexuality (by funding Gay Pride floats and rainbow-coloured high-speed trains, for instance). Corporate philanthropy works in the same way. It promotes 'CA', i.e. contemporary 'conceptual' art, and humanitarian associations that advocate the most conformist causes. Some large retailers—such as Truffaut or Éram shoes, for example—even encourage their customers to be 'generous' by asking them to top up their bills by donating small amounts to (carefully) pre-selected charities. It is a clever way to boost their publicity by making others pay for their (targeted) 'generosity'… Yielding to campaigns conducted by the Sleeping Giants, a far-left digital militia, many companies also intend to control their customers' opinions by depriving certain dissident media of advertisements, shutting down fundraising campaigns (Leetchi), and refusing to open bank accounts. In the process, companies are implementing outright professional bans, leading to dismissals for political reasons. The tweet police are everywhere and innocent Facebook posts can be used by business thugs as a prosecution tool. A further threshold has been crossed with the implementation of private censorship by GAFA. This censorship offers neither the guarantee of a fair debate nor any sort of recourse, which represents a tremendous regression of our freedom of expression. By submitting to the dictatorship of small, active minorities who enforce their demands through terror, many companies are becoming instruments of cancel culture, i.e. of the culture of cancellation and erasure.

The Rule of Law: The New Stone Tablets

Originally, the rule of law was a neutral concept which meant that a country respected the hierarchy of norms: the constitution, laws, and regulations. This concept was gradually subverted by judges (European and local alike) who established themselves as politically correct interpreters of general texts (constitution preambles, European treaties, or other international texts). This development was supported by both the media and many law universities, all of which were eager to reinforce their power. Thus, what should be the subject of political debate (the issues of immigration, minority rights, and even environmental policies) was eradicated from the scope of free discussion to empower the progressive doctrine: the notion of having 'no right to say or even think such things, because it's against the law' has become a classic rhetorical device. Interpreted in such a manner, the 'law' is transformed into new stone tablets.

The judicial agenda is also used to shape public opinion by publicising certain cases through high-profile trials, while obscuring others. Public opinion is thus presented with a biased representation of reality. In France, the accidental death of far-left activist Méric during a brawl he himself had provoked was the subject of several high-profile trials, allowing the 'far right' to be demonised. However, in the case of Philippe Monguillot, a bus driver beaten to death by a group of thugs, the investigating judge chose to deliberately downplay the facts.

In 2015, the Bataclan massacre became the largest Islamist attack in Europe. In 2021–2022, the justice system organised a spectacular nine-month trial, less to establish the known facts than to achieve a collective catharsis in the mindset of a White March.[27] It was a judicial smokescreen designed to divert attention from the Islamist nature of the attack, while simultaneously pushing the various victims and civil parties to unite in a stance of compulsory forgiveness and declare: 'You

---

27 TN: The expression 'White March' originally referred to the demonstrations that followed the arrest of serial killer and child molester Marc Dutroux in Belgium.

will not arouse my hatred.' One of the victims, François, attested to the psychological pressure he had suffered:

> After the attacks, there was a sort of injunction for us not to harbour hatred; for us not to stoop to a lower level. And at first, I told myself that I was very happy about that. But actually, yes, I do hate them. I definitely hate them. And I'm not ashamed of it. It's normal. I hate all the ones who took those many lives, destroyed countless others, and tried to take more, including mine. I still carry a simmering anger deep inside myself.

Alas, not everyone reacts similarly: for example, Jesse Hughes, the singer of the Eagles of Death Metal, chose to testify at the trial to show that he had fallen back in line, despite having questioned the Arab-Muslim security at the Bataclan in the immediate aftermath. This is obviously anything but neutral: it is simply a matter of prohibiting the expression of 'bad thoughts' (Orwell), especially when it comes to naming one's enemy, denouncing the danger of political Islam, and resisting it.

This instrumentalisation of the justice system is not unique to France. In Great Britain, the rape and enslavement of young White girls at the hands of Pakistani gangs was long covered up by the police. When a trial did ultimately take place, however, it was held behind closed doors, and whistleblower Tommy Robinson served several months in prison for having simply spoken out. And this happened in the land of the *Magna Carta* (1214), the *Habeas Corpus* (1679), and the Bill of Rights (1689)…

Controlled Politicians

The principle of democracy lies in the people's free choice, a choice that must also be adequately informed. And all political parties must have equal access to voters through the media. This, however, is not the case. Parties that inscribe their approach into the accepted *doxa* and relay the latter further enjoy privileged access to the media and play on home turf. On the other hand, their populist opponents often face hostile refuters who criticise them polemically, which results in their being judged as… aggressive. And that's the first bias.

The second bias is even more significant. And it goes like this: if you attach particular importance to a specific struggle, such as the defence of your identity, traditional values, sovereignty, etc., it is tempting to compensate for the hostility that you arouse in one domain (immigration, societal laws, criticism of the European Union or foreign policies, etc.) with extreme wariness, or even complacency, on other issues. Far from fighting against the propaganda society, many political actors thus contribute to strengthening it. Because, in order to defend a position that is hostile to the orthodoxy on point A, they think it clever to reinforce it on points B, C, and D. The defenders of the *doxa* thus divide and conquer while their opponents surrender to bickering. To give an example, some of the elected members of the AfD, a German sovereigntist and identity-based party, aligned themselves with NATO positions during the Russo-Ukrainian War in the hope of gaining greater media access.

The ones that champion such an attitude are, generally speaking, autonomist, even pro-independence, parties, attached to the identity of Scotland, Catalonia, or Corsica, for instance; autonomists that rage against London, Madrid or Paris while simultaneously extolling the idea of 'living together' with those that come from the depths of Africa or the Arab-Muslim world. Catalan nationalists take this approach to the extreme: they display bitter hostility towards Spanish people and the language of Cervantes while claiming to be very open to immigration from the Third World in the name of 'coexistence' and rejecting 'hate speech'. The Corsican 'nationalists' are not to be outdone, either: when Yvan Colonna, who had been serving a prison sentence for the assassination of Prefect Érignac, was strangled by a fellow inmate in the name of Allah, his supporters denounced the 'murderous French state' rather than the Islamists. Moreover, those who rose up against the Muslim privatisation of a beach in Sisco or the stoning of firefighters at the Jardins de l'Empereur housing project in Ajaccio were civilians and not their pro-autonomy representatives, whose response was very timid indeed. In short, due to practical constraints, opportunistic prudence, or conformity, political representatives reinforce rather than challenge the orthodoxy of the propaganda society.

Last but not least, there is a third bias that allows the *doxa* to control political expression, namely the choice of debated topics during electoral campaigns. During the 2021 German legislative elections, identity and security issues were neglected in favour of economic, social and environmental ones. In the 2022 French presidential campaign, and against the backdrop of the Russo-Ukrainian War, the issue of 'purchasing power' was brought to the forefront in an attempt to sidestep the issues of the Great Replacement and immigrant savagery. Indeed, the propaganda society only tolerates a truncated and rigged democracy — a post-democracy.

Facing the Mulag[28]: Dissent, Rebellion, and Secession

Forty years ago, it was common to contrast the 'free world', symbolised by the West at the time, with the Soviet Union or the land of gulags. However, although the USSR liberalised itself before disappearing, it is in the West that conformism became increasingly oppressive, shifting from soft ideology (François-Bernard Huygue, 1987) to soft totalitarianism (Rod Dreher, 2021). It's a sort of 'mulag', a mental gulag usually devoid of prisons — except in exceptional cases — but characterised by increasing censorship in our public and everyday life and by the rise of professional prohibitions. Perhaps even more serious is the evolution towards an increasingly sanitised society, marked not only by political conformism, but also by a decline in knowledge and intelligence, existential emptiness, general passivity, and reluctance to make any sort of effort. So how are we to cope with this? How can we move from dissidence to secession and from secession to reconquest?

---

28 TN: A mental gulag.

Rebellion? Having a Rebel Heart

The Norman (and dissident) writer Jean Mabire had come to terms with the limits of his struggle:

> We will not change the world; we must not delude ourselves. However, although we are not the ones who could transform this world, the latter will not change us, either.

As for Dominique Venner, 'to exist is to fight what denies me. Being a rebel is not a matter of collecting irreverent books and dreaming of phantasmagorical plots or resistance movements in the Cévennes. To be a rebel is to embody one's own standard; to stand by oneself no matter the cost. It is to ensure that one never recovers from their youthfulness, to rather alienate everyone else than be made to grovel, [...] and in setbacks, never to question the futility of a lost battle.'

Anchoring Oneself by Returning to the Humanities

And to achieve this, one must anchor oneself. To strive to 'live according to our tradition is to conform to the ideal that it embodies, cultivating excellence in relation to one's nature, rediscovering one's roots, transmitting one's heritage, and showing solidarity with one's own people' (Venner). And to anchor oneself, one must cultivate different types of memory: historical memory, social memory, and cultural memory. This requires a return to the humanities, both for oneself and for one's children: the discovery or rediscovery of history, philosophy, the great literary texts, tales in their ancient and unadulterated form, and classic films, i.e. those of the 'world before'. One thinks of Ernst Jünger in this regard:

> Perhaps at the end of this century [the 20th], we shall distinguish two categories of men: some formed by television and others by their reading.

Behaviour and Attitude: *Mens Sana in Corpore Sano*

The old Latin maxim 'A healthy mind in a healthy body' retains all its relevance, for it is a school of behaviour: fewer screens, more books; less virtuality, more reality. To avoid being benumbed by the world, one turns to forests (Jünger): walking, hunting, hiking, and *the dark paths* (Tesson[29]); confronting both nature and life through risky sports (mountaineering, horse riding, parachuting, hang-gliding, diving); endurance events (marathons, trail running), team sports (rugby), combat sports (boxing), and shooting. And for the youngest ones (one hundred and fifty thousand are involved each year), there is scouting, a wonderful school of life that allows one to evade any slackening and obesity, particularly when donning the strict uniforms of the Scouts Unitaires de France (SUF), the Scouts of Europe, the Scouts of Europe-Youth, or the Scouts Randonneurs.[30] In short, one must fight against 'lethal lukewarmness' (Konrad Lorenz[31]).

Such are the personal prerequisites for one to elude the 'mental occupation forces' (Laurent Ozon[32]) of this propaganda society. For this to occur, however, dissent must lead to secession.

Secession

Media-Related Secession

Secession is primarily media-based and consists in exercising one's critical thinking to gain a better perspective on progressive whims and the manipulative ploys used by the media and the cultural and entertainment industries. To be understood, all information must be processed and deciphered. Everything we read, everything we listen

---

29 TN: Sylvain Tesson is a French author and traveller.
30 TN: Literally 'rambling scouts'.
31 TN: Konrad Lorenz was an Austrian zoologist and ethologist.
32 TN: A French essayist and political activist.

to, and everything we watch must therefore be questioned and put into an appropriate historical, scientific, or statistical perspective. Every event must be considered not through a single truth but from different, complementary and sometimes even contradictory perspectives. For this purpose, having access to alternative media is invaluable, especially since today's fake news is often tomorrow's truth. Faced with the most blatant lies of this propaganda society, laughter is actually liberating. Particularly since propaganda is not all-powerful in the face of the shock of reality: everyone knows, for instance, that the expression 'young person' is, in fact, an allusion to an African or Maghrebi individual, and that a 'working-class neighbourhood' is an area with a high concentration of immigrants.

Media-related secession, however, is obviously insufficient.

Territorial Secession

To Yann Vallerie, who authored a notable work entitled *Secession*, only close-knit and deeply rooted communities will have the capacity to resist the edicts of the 'replacement state' (Renaud Camus) and the propaganda society. This leads the author to advocate territorial secession, which consists in 'fleeing the metropolises and settling in rural areas and medium-sized towns on a mass scale' in order to rediscover nature, occupy that space, and reconnect with community life.

Educational Secession

Educational secession is the natural complement of territorial secession, since official education no longer teaches anything but, instead, seeks merely to re-educate young French and European children, so as to make them accept their own downfall and to impose political correctness in the minds of future voters. For this reason, it constantly attacks families, particularly under the pretext of fighting Islamist 'separatism' or protecting 'children's rights'. 'Secession through education' thus amounts to rejecting this model by once again fleeing metropolitan areas, strengthening parental control over schools, and opting for/supporting independent education or homeschooling, while simultaneously re-establishing the educational role of parents.

Political Secession

Political secession consists in directly opposing progressive forces and the dictatorship of activist minorities: in the face of the *mulag*, we must wage an ideological battle to shift the Overton window completely to the right! This is indeed possible: whatever the case, it's what the Hungarian and Polish governments and American conservatives are now doing.

CHAPTER III

FROM SECESSION TO RECONQUEST

SHIFTING THE OVERTON WINDOW ALL THE WAY TO THE RIGHT

A Terrifying Tyranny — What Can Be Done?

FACED WITH THIS terrifying advance of tyranny, there are three possible attitudes to adopt:

- To contribute to the sustained shifting of the Overton window in the direction of wokeist and 'progressive' values, which is what many university students, minority group activists and politicians (ranging from Macron to Mélenchon[1]) are actually doing, thus embodying the two faces of progressivism: progressivism in motion and progressivism in accelerated motion.

- Not to rock the boat and to consider irreversible the continued shifting of the Overton window in the direction of deconstructionist delusions; to regard the latter as inevitabilities and accept them

---

1   TN: Born on 19 August 1951, Jean-Luc Mélenchon is a French politician who can only be described as left-wing or far-leftist.

as new benchmarks for 'reasonable' action: such is the attitude that prevails in the great quagmire where 'moderate' administrative, business and media elites come together. To them, all that would have belonged to their parents' realm of irrationality has now become an element of the sphere of reason. This is also the attitude espoused by the main European political parties that are presented as 'right-wing', but whose guiding principle is 'never to rock the boat'.

- To reject this entire situation and, instead, attempt to shift the Overton window towards the values of freedom, identity and conservatism. This is what some courageous university students, dissident think tanks, alternative media and a number of political parties (including Reconquête in France, Vox in Spain, Vlaams Belang in Belgium, the AfD in Germany, and Fratelli d'Italia) are attempting to do at all costs.

Incidentally, it is important to realise one thing: anyone who regards the current opening of the Overton window as an irreversible development must accept the fact that, in the future, it could once again be shifted towards new delusions. And the only way to avoid the latter is to undertake to radically reshift the Overton window towards new horizons!

Hard right rudder, then, my friends, for there can be no half-hearted measures!

We must no longer tolerate the ever more delusional shifting of the Overton window. What we must do instead is undertake to break entirely with the madness of progressivism and wokeism. What follows is a twenty-one-point programme towards achieving this very purpose.

1. Identify the Enemy: Minority Lobbies

The enemy is embodied by the activist minorities of minority lobbies and subsidised associations, regardless of whether they are 'anti-racist', pro-immigration, feminist, or LGBTQ. The same goes for the powers that support them: davocracy,[2] the Soros constellation, the Anglo-Saxon deep state, GAFA (Big Tech) companies, and the mainstream media. We must denounce progressivism as a totalitarian and violent ideology upheld by lunatics and those that wreak destruction.

2. Reaffirm Fundamental European Values in the Face of the Deconstructionists

We must strive to reaffirm the right of European nations to civilisational identity and historical continuity, while contrasting our pride in a prestigious past (from which the entire world has benefited) with the foulness of exaggerated repentance against the backdrop of World War II, colonisation and slavery, or even that of imported North American racial conflicts.

Europe is the civilisation of realisation, freedom and remarkable discoveries; a civilisation that respects women and recognises the divine in nature. Let us all be proud of it!

3. Champion the Beautiful

Championing beauty means re-introducing the latter into one's decision-making criteria while fighting against the excesses of techno-managerial logic and quantitative thinking, both of which refuse to take into account anything that doesn't fit into an Excel spreadsheet. It also implies opposing any relativism that promotes ugliness and deconstruction in the fields of clothing, street furniture, destructuralised architecture, and so-called contemporary art. To defend beauty is to take into consideration the principles of natural attractiveness, as well as the concern for harmony of shape, colour and symmetry, while also retaining the aesthetic canons of the great works as one's reference.

---

2 TN: Davocracy refers to the rule and activities of the World Economic Forum, an international non-governmental organisation and think tank based in Cologny, Canton of Geneva, Switzerland.

4. Remain Steadfast in the Face of Any Attack Against Our Freedom of Expression

Since the dawn of Greek culture, freedom of debate has been the foundation of European civilisation.

In European culture, and outside all religious dogma, only that which can be freely debated can be said to be true. This rule lies at the very origin of scientific development and the foundations of democracy, with the latter having first been established in *agoras*[3] and forums, terms that are still so very present today! Without debates, it is obscurantism which prevails, along with the dictatorship of interests that are based on lies. One does not 'regulate' freedom of expression; one defends it tooth and nail as being one of the pillars of our world.

5. Never Submit, Never Give In, and Impose Reciprocity

Do not submit; do not give in; do not allow yourself to be victimised; do not remain silent; and always state what you believe: everywhere — both on public platforms and in private conversations with friends, family and colleagues, during which you must not surrender to conformity. Everyone can avoid addressing certain topics to ward off controversy, but as soon as contentious subjects are raised, the plurality of viewpoints must be respected. There can be no unilateral disarmament — no 'woke' speech without identity speech; no 'progressive' talk without conservative talk; and no oligarchic discourse without populist discourse. Such is the notion of reciprocity.

6. Denounce Untruths, Point Out All Denials of What Is Real, and Transgress

No, gender differences are not mere social constructs, as their roots are, in fact, biological; just like the differences between peoples, which are not only cultural but also of genetic origin. And no, there is no

---

3   TN: Ancient Greek marketplaces or, from our more contemporary perspective, gathering places.

such thing as a 'pregnant man', nor is there any systemic racism among white people.

There is, however, a systemic over-delinquency present among ethnic minorities in Western countries. And this has been statistically proven.

As for any differences in academic and professional success between ethnic groups, they are due to heredity rather than the environment, as demonstrated by numerous studies, particularly on people's intelligence quotient (IQ).

Let us not accept convention-based compromises under the pretext of not offending anyone. Let us instead transgress.

7. Call All Inconsistencies into Question

The totalitarians that govern us campaign for 'non-discrimination', yet they encourage 'civic discrimination' on social media, at universities and in businesses against anyone who would express non-conformist views. Any criticism of immigration is deemed 'racist' or 'xenophobic', although the persecution of Russians, including Russian artists, has been encouraged in the wake of the Russo-Ukrainian War. And what about healthcare access discrimination targeting those who did not get vaccinated against COVID-19, including healthcare workers and ill people? As for environmental problems, they are not limited to the sole issue of global warming. And if it is anthropogenic and due to carbon emissions, why have we fought so hard against nuclear energy, which is quintessentially carbon-free? Last but not least, it remains astonishing to see people promoting both feminism and Islamisation, or zealously meticulous gender equality on the one hand and Sharia law on the other... Just as it is strange to witness people's obsession with school inclusion for all children with disabilities, when 95% to 98% of all embryos with Down syndrome will not have the opportunity to be included in schools, since they are expelled from their mother's womb.

8. Denounce the Nefariousness of the Progressivists

We must not be fooled, however, for behind the apparent contradictions of progressivism lies a common thread: the desire to trap European civilisation in a pincer movement. To endorse Islamisation on the one hand while also discouraging higher ethnic birth rates is to advocate the Great Replacement. Fighting discrimination and implementing 'positive discrimination', which is only positive to some, means oppressing the majority for the benefit of certain minorities.

Progressivists are not inconsistent: they are simply evil, and it is this evil that must be fought against. Indeed, progressivism is not synonymous with generous action — it is, instead, a destructive, totalitarian, and violent ideology that must be denounced.

9. Counter-Demonise the Demonisers

The enemy's strategy is to demonise — and then render invisible — those who would defend continuity and identity. It is not enough for us to take blows with gritted teeth. We must, in fact, counterattack by denouncing the deconstructionists, the demolitionists, the vassals of Americanisation, those subservient to Islamisation, and all sectarian censors. We must no longer speak of (unpleasant) 'anti-fascists' but of violent far-left militias (which reflects reality far more accurately). We must (symbolically) strike against all those moralisers — whether athletes, artists, or academics — who play the risk-free part of political correctness petitioners, as they are the ones who enjoy all the publicity, while a former Miss France is ostracised for expressing her electoral preference for Éric Zemmour.[4]

10. Boycott the Advocates of Progressivism

Some companies are now engaging in zealous wokeism either by depriving dissident media and alternative social media accounts from

---

[4] TN: Described by his opponents as a far-right politician, Éric Justin Léon Zemmour is also active as an essayist, writer, and political journalist.

the opportunity to share their views, or by imposing their own whims in their advertising messages, which promote 'creolisation' and the abolition of gender differences.

One must therefore do whatever it takes to remove them from one's purchase and follow lists and conduct campaigns to destabilise those that run them. Let us rejoice at the misfortunes of Netflix, whose particularly heavy-handed woke propaganda drove many customers away, leading to a drop in stock market value. And in the United States, Disney's popularity ratings plummeted from 77% to 33% after its CEO declared that she wanted a minimum of 50% LGBTQIA and 'racialised' characters in its various series.

11. No Mercy for the Pigeon-Hearted!

Let us be clear here: progressivism and wokeism only prevail because of the weakness of those that hold economic, political, and media power and who, due to their cowardice, lack the courage to oppose them both. We must therefore counter-pressure them, never allowing them to rest.

It is all for their own good, of course, because anyone whose identity is deconstructed today is doomed to be a *dhimmi*[5] tomorrow!

12. Be Ironic and Resort to Liberating Laughter

We must mock conformists and target with irony all those who promote their orthodoxy in the form of banners on social media: first 'I am Charlie',[6] then suddenly the COVID-19 vaccination syringe, and next the Ukrainian flag.

Refuse to take fraudulent academic studies seriously and ridicule the experts that support them. Show no reverence for the insanity of conceptual art and burst into loud liberating laughter.

---

5   TN: The term *dhimmi* refers to 'protected' non-Muslims living under Islamic rule.

6   TN: In reference to the Charlie Hebdo massacre.

13. Reject Unilateral Disarmament: Embrace Vital Violence

Whether on university premises or during street demonstrations, violent far-left militias impose their vile rule by force, terrorising students and professors and thus undermining people's freedom of opinion, or seizing upon and hijacking the Yellow Vest movement, a popular movement thus sent spiralling towards a dead end. We must be able to confront this violence, or to be more precise, take it upon ourselves to confront it in the media: there is no shame in defending our freedom of assembly, expression, and movement — on the contrary! And we must do so with our fists if necessary. In the face of such attacks, we must assert our right to self-defence. We thus salute the new generation of activists who have understood this! Let us therefore not fail to support them.

14. No (Financial) Quarter for Freedom-Destroying Sectarians

Activist minorities attack our freedoms while draining our funds. We must track down the subsidies they receive at every administrative level: in various municipalities, departments, and regions, as well as within the state and the European Union. We must, furthermore, exert pressure on our political authorities to cut off the financial taps. And as regards the print media and public broadcasting, we must fight to put an end to their public funding, since they do not respect pluralism.

More generally, we must campaign for the ideological and political rebalancing of the media, so that conservatives and Identitarians can reclaim their rightful place. This presupposes, as done by Bolloré[7] with certain French media outlets (and Elon Musk with Twitter/X), a certain house-cleaning process. There can always be 'woke' people and progressivists, of course, but on the condition that they do not enjoy

---

7   TN: Vincent Bolloré is a French billionaire businessman who has used his media influence to allow rightist politicians such as Zemmour to enjoy equal prominence as their leftist opponents.

(almost) complete monopoly and do not impose anything on others. Besides, since these people are conducting a purge within their own ranks, it would be quite logical for them to leave a little space for those who do not think the way they do.

15. Advocate the Right to Preference in the Name of Freedom

It is futile to complain about discrimination and fight it for an illusory sort of equality. On the contrary, we must demand to be granted the right to preference in the name of freedom. Yes, we must be able to choose who we would want as a colleague, employee, or (co-)tenant: a man rather than a woman (or vice versa), a white person over a black person (or vice versa), a mother over a transsexual on testosterone (or vice versa), a Catholic over a Muslim (or vice versa)… It's a matter of choice, a matter of preference, and a matter of freedom!

16. Stay Positive: Praise the Beautiful and the Good

In the face of the steamroller of a single ideology, one risks becoming grumpy or even cranky. Although this can indeed be the result of an attitude of resistance, refusing to surrender is not just about 'fighting what denies us': it is also about spreading and promoting all that supports the values of identity and freedom, conservatism, and continuity. '*It is better to light a candle than curse the darkness*' (Lao Tzu) and, therefore, to praise all that is beautiful and good, whether in children's books or in literary, cinematographic, musical and video productions. It should particularly be noted that museum libraries are often exceptionally stocked and that highway rest areas sometimes allow for wonderful discoveries.

17. Rediscover the Meaning of Words

Academician Andrei Makine believes that 'the French novel will only regain its lost vigour by embracing words that allow us to grasp reality rather than mask it.' Let us therefore rediscover the meaning of words.

Let us do away with *Frenglish*, Newspeak and techno-managerial terminology, while respecting the rules of grammar and saving the use of punctuation and capital letters. Let us rediscover the 'subtleties of contemporary French' (Renaud Camus) and prefer distinction to indistinctness.

18. International Solidarity: Anti-Wokeists Worldwide, Unite!

The Overton window has not only been moved in France, but also throughout the Western world (including Western Europe, North America, Australia, and New Zealand); a Western world that is becoming the laughingstock of the entire world: BRICS countries (Brazil, Russia, India, China, South Africa), which represent the majority of the world's population, thus mock the Western world's pretension to impose its 'values' upon the world, when the latter are based on its own self-denigration.

In every country of the Western world, however, there are some who resist progressivism and wokeism: such is the case of the Dissident Right in the United States, of Identitarian and populist movements in Western Europe, and the conservative governments of Hungary and Poland. They must therefore apply Mao Zedong's motto of 'marching separately, but striking together!'

19. Resist

Just as 'believe, obey, fight' was the motto of fascism, ours must be: 'doubt, disobey, resist.'

20. Hard Right Rudder!

So, are you ready to move the Overton window once again and start a peaceful discussion on the topic of remigration? Are you ready to reconsider, without any taboos, the issue of the death penalty and the founding of a sovereign state?

Are you ready to open a debate on the necessary regulation of abortion, to put an end to surrogacy for all women, to break the hold of pedagogical zealots and reinstate a selection process in schools and universities? Are you ready to cut off the financial taps that fuel progressive associations, to restore genuine freedom of expression and protect our environment and landscapes at the risk of displeasing climate alarmists? Are you ready to rediscover pride in your own past without unduly blushing in the face of history books? Are you? Then now is the time!

21. Stay Strong! Stay Strong! Stay Strong!

Our last commandment can be summed up in one phrase: Stay strong!

Courage is the necessary virtue for peoples to endure through history.

Courage is the necessary virtue for men to stand fast.

And courage will be required to once more move the Overton window: moral courage to transgress the new taboos, physical courage to no longer leave the streets in the hands of aggressive minorities, and serene courage for us all — for *'only cowards shy away from combat.'* (Homer)

L'INSTITUT ILIADE FOR LONG EUROPEAN MEMORY

L'Institut Iliade for Long European Memory, based in France, was born from an observation. Europe is but a shadow of her former self. Replaced by outsiders, confused by having lost their bearing and their pride, Europeans have abandoned the reins of their common destiny to people other than themselves. Europeans no longer remember. Why? Because amongst the current elite — whether at school, university, or in the media — no one passes down to them the cultural wealth of which they are the inheritors.

Contrary to this moribund current, L'Institut Iliade has given itself the task of participating in the renewal of the cultural grandeur of Europe and in aiding Europeans' reappropriation of their own identity. Facing the Great Erasure of culture, we intend to work for the Great Awakening of European consciousness and to help prepare Europe for a new renaissance — one of identity, freedom, and power.

L'Institut Iliade's calling is threefold:

- To train young men and young women concerned about their history to always build. To make them the avantgarde of the renaissance for which the Institut calls: men and women capable of giving to civic and political action that cultural and metapolitical dimension which is indispensable. Their motto: to put themselves at the service of a community of destiny, which risks disappearing if it is not taken in hand. Armed with a strong culture relating to European traditions and values, they learn to discern that the adventure that awaits them entails risks and self-sacrifice, but also enthusiasm and joy.

- To promote a radical and alternative vision of the world contrary to the dogmas of universalism, egalitarianism, and 'diversity'. Using all available means, the Institut develops concepts and ammunition to understand and fight the modern world.
- To gather together, especially — but not only — in France, those who refuse to submit and who are inspired daily by the Homeric triad as described by Dominique Venner: nature as the base, excellence as the goal, beauty as the horizon.

L'Institut Iliade's originality, especially with the aim of reformulating and updating knowledge, lies in tying together the seriousness of its content with ease of learning for the greater public, the objective being to demonstrate an authentic pedagogy, and to act in complementary or supportive ways with other initiatives having the same goal.

L'Institut Iliade's action takes place across various channels:

- A cadre school of the European Rebirth, which every year brings together trainees from a wide variety of backgrounds and is already seeing citizens from other European countries participate;
- an annual colloquium — made up of academics, politicians, writers, journalists, and association officials from all over Europe — that meets in Paris to discuss strong and challenging themes, such as 'The Aesthetic Universe of Europeans', 'Facing the Migratory

Assault', 'Transmit or Disappear', 'Nature as Base — for an Ecology of Place', 'Beyond the Market — Economy at the Service of Peoples';

- the publication of works — designed as beacons to enlighten readers' thoughts and guide them toward the reconquest of their identity — within several collections, made available in the widest array of languages and European countries;
- artistic exhibitions on the fringes of contemporary artistic trends, allowing the public to take a fresh look at art and rooted creation;
- an incubator for ideas, businesses, and associations to support and help the greatest number of projects — with quality and sustainability criteria — across all fields of civil society (culture, commerce, etc.) that seek to impose a rooted vision of the world and an alternative to the current system, while prioritising structures and projects making an impact in real life;
- an active presence on social media, allowing us to reach new audiences (through videos, publications, annual events, and news presentations), centred around a website that functions as much as a resource hub as it does as a platform for exchanges and debate, notably offering an ideal library of more than five hundred works, a European primer, a dictionary of quotations, and turnkey itineraries for visiting and hiking the prominent places of European memory.

Education through history:

L'Institut Iliade endeavours to uphold in every circumstance the richness and singularity of our heritage in order to draw forth the source and the resources of a serene, but determined, affirmation of our identity, both national and European. In line with the thought and deeds of Dominique Venner, the Institut accords in all its activities an essential place to history, both as a matrix of deep meditation on the future as well as a place of the unexpected, where anything is possible.

Concerning Europe, it seems as though we will be forced to rise up and face immense challenges and fearsome catastrophes even beyond those posed by immigration. These hardships will present the opportunity for both a rebirth and a rediscovery of ourselves. I believe in those qualities that are specific to the European people, qualities currently in a state of dormancy. I believe in our active individuality, our inventiveness, and in the awakening of our energy. This awakening will undoubtedly come. When? I do not know, but I am positive that it will take place.

— Dominique Venner, *The Shock of History*
Arktos Media, London, 2015

Follow L'Institut Iliade at
www.institut-iliade.com
linktr.ee/InstitutILIADE

OTHER BOOKS PUBLISHED BY ARKTOS

Virginia Abernethy	Born Abroad
Sri Dharma Pravartaka Acharya	The Dharma Manifesto
Joakim Andersen	Rising from the Ruins
Winston C. Banks	Excessive Immigration
Stephen Baskerville	Who Lost America?
Alfred Baeumler	Nietzsche: Philosopher and Politician
Matt Battaglioli	The Consequences of Equality
Alain de Benoist	Beyond Human Rights
	Carl Schmitt Today
	The Ideology of Sameness
	The Indo-Europeans
	Manifesto for a European Renaissance
	On the Brink of the Abyss
	The Problem of Democracy
	Runes and the Origins of Writing
	View from the Right (vol. 1–3)
Armand Berger	Tolkien, Europe, and Tradition
Pawel Bielawski	European Apostasy
Arthur Moeller van den Bruck	Germany's Third Empire
Kerry Bolton	The Perversion of Normality
	Revolution from Above
	Yockey: A Fascist Odyssey
Isac Boman	Money Power
Charles William Dailey	The Serpent Symbol in Tradition
Antoine Dresse	Political Realism
Ricardo Duchesne	Faustian Man in a Multicultural Age
Alexander Dugin	Ethnos and Society
	Ethnosociology
	Eurasian Mission
	The Fourth Political Theory
	The Great Awakening vs the Great Reset
	Last War of the World-Island
	Politica Aeterna
	Political Platonism
	Putin vs Putin
	The Rise of the Fourth Political Theory
	The Trump Revolution
	Templars of the Proletariat
	The Theory of a Multipolar World
Daria Dugina	A Theory of Europe
Edward Dutton	Race Differences in Ethnocentrism
Mark Dyal	Hated and Proud
Clare Ellis	The Blackening of Europe
Koenraad Elst	Return of the Swastika
Julius Evola	The Bow and the Club
	Fascism Viewed from the Right
	A Handbook for Right-Wing Youth
	Metaphysics of Power

OTHER BOOKS PUBLISHED BY ARKTOS

	Metaphysics of War
	The Myth of the Blood
	Notes on the Third Reich
	Pagan Imperialism
	Recognitions
	A Traditionalist Confronts Fascism
GUILLAUME FAYE	*Archeofuturism*
	Archeofuturism 2.0
	The Colonisation of Europe
	Convergence of Catastrophes
	Ethnic Apocalypse
	A Global Coup
	Prelude to War
	Sex and Deviance
	Understanding Islam
	Why We Fight
DANIEL S. FORREST	*Suprahumanism*
ANDREW FRASER	*Dissident Dispatches*
	Reinventing Aristocracy in the Age of Woke Capital
	The WASP Question
GÉNÉRATION IDENTITAIRE	*We are Generation Identity*
PETER GOODCHILD	*The Taxi Driver from Baghdad*
	The Western Path
PAUL GOTTFRIED	*War and Democracy*
PETR HAMPL	*Breached Enclosure*
PORUS HOMI HAVEWALA	*The Saga of the Aryan Race*
CONSTANTIN VON HOFFMEISTER	*Esoteric Trumpism*
	MULTIPOLARITY!
RICHARD HOUCK	*Liberalism Unmasked*
A. J. ILLINGWORTH	*Political Justice*
INSTITUT ILIADE	*For a European Awakening*
	Guardians of Heritage
ALEXANDER JACOB	*De Naturae Natura*
JASON REZA JORJANI	*Artemis Unveiled*
	Closer Encounters
	Erosophia
	Faustian Futurist
	Iranian Leviathan
	Lovers of Sophia
	Metapolemos
	Novel Folklore
	Philosophy of the Future
	Prometheism
	Promethean Pirate
	Prometheus and Atlas
	Psychotron
	Uber Man
	World State of Emergency

OTHER BOOKS PUBLISHED BY ARKTOS

Henrik Jonasson	Sigmund
Edgar Julius Jung	The Significance of the German Revolution
Ruuben Kaalep & August Meister	Rebirth of Europe
Roderick Kaine	Smart and SeXy
James Kirkpatrick	Conservatism Inc.
Ludwig Klages	The Biocentric Worldview
	Cosmogonic Reflections
	The Science of Character
Andrew Korybko	Hybrid Wars
Pierre Krebs	Guillaume Faye: Truths & Tributes
	Fighting for the Essence
Julien Langella	Catholic and Identitarian
John Bruce Leonard	The New Prometheans
Diana Panchenko	The Inevitable
Stephen Pax Leonard	The Ideology of Failure
	Travels in Cultural Nihilism
William S. Lind	Reforging Excalibur
	Retroculture
Pentti Linkola	Can Life Prevail?
Giorgio Locchi	Definitions
H. P. Lovecraft	The Conservative
Norman Lowell	Imperium Europa
Richard Lynn	Sex Differences in Intelligence
	A Tribute to Helmut Nyborg (ed.)
John MacLugash	The Return of the Solar King
Charles Maurras	The Future of the Intelligentsia &
	For a French Awakening
Graeme Maxton	The Follies of the Western Mind
John Harmon McElroy	Agitprop in America
Michael O'Meara	Guillaume Faye and the Battle of Europe
	New Culture, New Right
Michael Millerman	Beginning with Heidegger
Dmitry Moiseev	The Philosophy of Italian Fascism
Maurice Muret	The Greatness of Elites
Brian Anse Patrick	The NRA and the Media
	Rise of the Anti-Media
	The Ten Commandments of Propaganda
	Zombology
Tito Perdue	The Bent Pyramid
	Journey to a Location
	Lee
	Morning Crafts
	Philip
	The Sweet-Scented Manuscript
	William's House (vol. 1–4)
John K. Press	The True West vs the Zombie Apocalypse

OTHER BOOKS PUBLISHED BY ARKTOS

Raido	*A Handbook of Traditional Living* (vol. 1–2)
P R Reddall	*Towards Awakening*
Claire Rae Randall	*The War on Gender*
Steven J. Rosen	*The Agni and the Ecstasy*
	The Jedi in the Lotus
Nicholas Rooney	*Talking to the Wolf*
Richard Rudgley	*Barbarians*
	Essential Substances
	Wildest Dreams
Ernst von Salomon	*It Cannot Be Stormed*
	The Outlaws
Werner Sombart	*Traders and Heroes*
Piero San Giorgio	*Giuseppe*
	Survive the Economic Collapse
	Surviving the Next Catastrophe
Sri Sri Ravi Shankar	*Celebrating Silence*
	Know Your Child
	Management Mantras
	Patanjali Yoga Sutras
	Secrets of Relationships
George T. Shaw (ed.)	*A Fair Hearing*
Oswald Spengler	*The Decline of the West*
	Man and Technics
Richard Storey	*The Uniqueness of Western Law*
J. R. Sommer	*The New Colossus*
Tomislav Sunic	*Against Democracy and Equality*
	Homo Americanus
	Postmortem Report
	Titans are in Town
Askr Svarte	*Gods in the Abyss*
Hans-Jürgen Syberberg	*On the Fortunes and Misfortunes of Art in Post-War Germany*
Abir Taha	*Defining Terrorism*
	The Epic of Arya (2nd ed.)
	Nietzsche is Coming God, or the Redemption of the Divine
	Verses of Light
Jean Thiriart	*Europe: An Empire of 400 Million*
Bal Gangadhar Tilak	*The Arctic Home in the Vedas*
Dominique Venner	*Ernst Jünger: A Different European Destiny*
	For a Positive Critique
	The Shock of History
Hans Vogel	*How Europe Became American*
Markus Willinger	*A Europe of Nations*
	Generation Identity
Alexander Wolfheze	*Alba Rosa*
	Globus Horribilis
	Rupes Nigra

Printed in Dunstable, United Kingdom